WOMEN'S LIBERATION AND THE CHURCH

WOMEN'S

AND

The New Demand for Freedom in

NEW YORK

LIBERATION

THE CHURCH

the Life of the Christian Church

Edited with Introduction by Sarah Bentley Doely

Published in Co-operation with IDOC–North America

ASSOCIATION PRESS

CONTENTS

For freedom Christ has set us free;
stand fast therefore, and do not submit
again to a yoke of slavery.

—Galatians 5:1, RSV

ACKNOWLEDGMENTS

I am indebted to all the contributors for their cooperation and their willingness to write on short notice. Circumstances prevented Nelle Morton, former professor of Christian Education at Drew Theological Seminary, from joining in our effort, but she was kind enough to share her bibliographical materials with me. Both she and Susan Barrabee were a welcome source of information and support. My deepest thanks go to Jack Becker of IDOC, who was always available when I needed him and who managed to combine the roles of editor, critic, "answer man," and friend with consistent warmth and good humor.

S.B.D.

INTRODUCTION

by Sarah Bentley Doely

At times it seems ironic to write about liberation. Liberation and the incredible experience of the freeing of the spirit seem somehow at odds with the constraining nature of the printed word. The greatest liberation story—the New Testament—was first spread directly, through word of mouth, by the disciples and friends of Christ who wished to tell the story of their new-found freedom.

After Pentecost the disciples, on a sort of "freedom high," told their story to anyone who would listen. They did not hesitate to include the doubts and fears which beset them as they struggled to live their beliefs. They testified to the saving power of Christ; they witnessed to the agony and triumph of his life with them; they told others again and again of the glorious new message of freedom which he had brought.

In the end the written word was necessary. The disciples traveled throughout the world, but they kept in contact with one another through letters. Paul guided the far-flung Christian communities through his letters. Stories of Jesus were collected and written down to be transmitted to eager peoples everywhere in an effort to convey the amazing experiences of the Incarnation, the Crucifixion and the Resurrection. Having been preserved, these are a written testament to the lively dialogue which dominated the life of the early church.

It is a Christian tradition to testify to one's convictions, to the presence of the Holy Spirit in one's life, to the saving power of Christ. It is in that tradition that this book should be read: as a written testament and a witness by women to their struggles to be truly free in the Christian church today. Perhaps the old meaning of the word *testify* best expresses this particular way of telling a story: "to make known, to give evidence." These chapters are an attempt to make known the experiences of women in the church and to share the concerns which have prompted the present questioning of woman's "place" in the church. The crucial need is to tell the story, to communicate what is happening in a variety of ways and places throughout the life of the church.

Women's liberation is abroad in the land; there can be no doubt about that. But too often it is stereotyped and caricatured by those —particularly the mass media—who see the possibility of exploiting it. The caricature of the ideas of this movement serves primarily to dull its cutting edge in society and to separate those who support it from those who, lacking the opportunity to see the issues in a different light, know only that they disagree with what they see on television and in much of the mass media. The story is being told, but only recently has it been told by those who know it and believe in it . . . and rarely by those within the church.

It is particularly important to make known this story to the women of the church so that those who have long expressed similar ideas will gain strength in having new support and those who have doubts can begin to understand what we're about. For the first time a dialogue may be established in local parishes and among the laity rather than in the predominantly male ecclesiastical bodies where it has frequently but often lightly (and with little result) been considered in the past.

The women who speak here are not casual onlookers of the church scene; each has been deeply involved in church life and her commitment to her faith is obvious. Equally obvious, however, are dissatisfactions, ranging in intensity from a desire for equal rights for women to an unequivocal "No" to the present values, norms and structures of the church. That these women bear a witness of love in demanding so passionately that the church take women seriously is true. Deep concern and honest faith have prompted them to speak out against an institution which receives their offers of commitment with difficulty and restraint. That they also speak, in varying degrees, with deep anger and resentment against the same church is equally true. Disappointment, disillusionment and profound criticism of the church are evident throughout these pages. It is the presence of both love and anger which makes it so difficult to disregard their message. Such bitter criticism is far more damning when offered by individuals who consider themselves in the church, and the anger which is most difficult to dismiss is that which is not born of petty disappointment, but of an insistence that the church be true to its own teachings of full humanity and new life for all.

What happens next? What do women want from the church? I leave it to the contributors to answer those questions in detail. But I would like to suggest here that the next move belongs to whomever takes it. *The response of the church is crucial.* Many ministers and denominational officials do not yet accept even a questioning of the role of women in the church. For example, some of those attending a recent conference of ministers held at Union Seminary did not feel that the workshop being held on women's liberation and the church even belonged on such a program.

Those who openly agree with them may be a minority, but an honest one at least. Many more, regardless of their sex, who pay lip service to the equal participation of men and women in the church have shown by their actions that they consider a few seats on the board of trustees or the "privilege" of ordination to be sufficient. It isn't. What is needed is the beginning of an open dialogue at all levels of church life and a willingness to listen to each other and honestly to confront the present subordinate status of women. We must all of us—men and women—talk as never before, and the church—which, after all, is all of us together—must listen as it has never listened before.

Equally crucial are the attitudes and actions which women will take in response to these questions. Will we speak or remain silent? Will we initiate dialogue or postpone it out of anxiety and fear? Will we listen to each other and respect the place where each of us stands? Will we comfort and support each other in each woman's effort to face the questions involved? And—if the answer from the church is "No"—will we be strong enough to leave privilege and pedestal behind and to follow our convictions to a new life with our brothers and sisters elsewhere?

Finally, will we be able to see through the present conflict to the new life we are seeking for ourselves and the church? Can we, as Peggy Way suggests, continue to call men "brother," even though they presently cannot call us "sister"? I am not suggesting that we play the role of "Aunt Jane" to the church fathers' Simon Legree, nor that we seek to reconcile ourselves at the cost of our full participation in the church. I am asking whether we can bring to this period of tension and conflict the unique compassion which is ours, not as *women,* but as *Christians.* The disharmony we must learn to live with, and that will be challenge enough for those of us who have always seen ourselves—and been seen by others—as the healers, the reconcilers, the peacemakers. We will have to believe in ourselves and what we are doing enough to live through the questioning of our very lives as women and as Christians. We will have to draw more fully than ever on our faith to see us through the divisions and hostilities which we have brought upon ourselves. But if we can do this—if we can struggle, with love, for the possibility of new life—we will certainly have understood the dual nature of the commandment to love our neighbors . . . *as we love ourselves.*

WOMEN'S LIBERATION AND THE CHURCH

by Davida Foy Crabtree

Since the first century, the church has been one of the chief oppressors of women by virtue of its hand-in-hand relationship with the world. While the Gospel affirms that Christians have a responsibility to stand over against the world when it poses its values as ultimate, yet the church has continually perpetuated the very social institutions, customs, and myths which it is called to criticize. With regard to the lives of women, the church has given rise and support to the myths of dependency and emotionality, the nuclear family system, the all-male Trinity. The values implied in these and other areas have worked to reinforce the cultural patterns which prevent women from living fulfilled lives. Thus the implications of the women's liberation movement for the church are both manifold and thoroughgoing.

In its most recent manifestation, the struggle for the release of women from their oppression has taken on a new and radically different conceptualization. Whereas the feminists of the early twentieth century saw their endeavor to be the gaining of "rights" or "suffrage" for American women, we in the last third of that same century see our cause as "liberation."

This movement for women's liberation must be seen as striving after not merely freedom *from* oppression, but equally and simultaneously freedom *for* new ways of living and new views of ourselves as full persons. Throughout the centuries, we women have been denied the right to determine our own lives on the grounds that we must be dependent on men for food and shelter since childbearing has left us in a weakened condition. We have been Adam's rib, John's wife and Herb's daughter, sex object and little old lady; but seldom have we been allowed to be whole persons with identities and personalities which are not rooted in another person (father, husband, child). Even less often have women been recorded in history as important and positive contributors to the building of cultures. We have been excluded from positions of authority and of power, from restaurants and voting booths, from pulpits and cockpits. And we ask why. At this point in history, as humans, we are technologically able to control our own lives. No longer can men point to our bodies and excuse their crude ascendency thereby, for in this century men have unwittingly provided the key for women's liberation: no longer must we bear unlimited numbers of children, and thereby confine ourselves to restricted participation in society. With increasing technologization, physical strength is a criterion for employment in few fields. Indeed, it often happens that the wife and mother who is at home all day exerts much more physical strength than does her husband at his work in office or factory.

It is this image and stereotype of woman as weak, dependent, hyperemotional, and nonintellectual which the women's liberation movement calls into question. The oppression of women in American society today is not limited to employment discrimination. On the contrary, sexism, like racism, so pervades our social structure, myths and categories that the success of our movement will result in a radical transformation of every aspect of our personal and collective lives. Thus, we assert that we must be freed from the cultural mentality which makes women sexy second-class citizens, the same mentality which claims that anatomy is destiny. In short, women in the women's liberation movement are in battle against those definitions of women that make us objects, seen as existing either on a pedestal or in the gutter—as the church would have it, either as the Virgin Mary or as Gomer. (Hosea 1:3)

It is precisely in the rebellion against conformity to the cultural norm that women have begun to be most articulate about their hopes, ideals, and goals for the future. While the movement may appear to the casual observer as having a purely negative thrust, in fact its orientation is constructive and full of hope. At the same time that these women are criticizing society, they are setting up models for new life styles through collectives, communes, and child-care centers. The principal aim is provision of a variety of options from which women can choose at any given point in their lives. Presently young girls do not really have a choice when they confront their own futures. The great majority of them are living in homes and communities where the "normal" woman spends all of her time at home caring for husband and children. If she works, it is regarded as temporary, and she is "only doing it for the family." There is only disdain and pity for any woman in the community who has remained single. One need only think of the different connotations of the terms *spinster* and *bachelor* to provide a graphic example of the vast difference in futures open to women and to men.

In the past, women have found themselves cut off from each other either through physical isolation in the single-family home or through an inbred distrust of other women which stems from the early days of competitive dating and education. Today, many are beginning to challenge these self-images by gathering in small, disciplined groups which meet regularly to share the profound experiences and thoughts which are part of their everyday lives as women. Those who have been part of such groups, known to them as collectives and familiar to us in the church as cell groups, have testified to their power in helping women overcome their fear and distrust of each other and themselves. Beyond that, such an experience has time and again revealed to individuals and groups that it is through our alienation from each other that we have been kept powerless. Conversely, participants in these groups have learned that it is not only possible but necessary for women to assert themselves collectively in society in order to overturn the "masculine" cultural values which presently predominate. Indeed, those values cannot be changed without first changing the societal institutions and structures which reinforce and mold attitudes. Recognizing that the women's liberation movement is for the most part in a dangerously personalistic phase at this time, yet we assert that such a stage is necessary to alert women to the issues and to weld a strong solidarity. From here we will move to more intense political action.

Thus the ideal society projected by women's liberation would be one in which women faced an open future in a cultural setting which enhanced their self-image and assured them of an identity in their own right. As a society, we would be co-operative rather than competitive. The cultural stereotypes of what is masculine and what is feminine would be eradicated and replaced by a new understanding of what is human. Menial tasks and decision-making power and responsibility would be shared so that all would participate in meaningful work. Social structures would be so transformed as to encourage the participation of all at every level of society.

While the women's liberation movement is a struggle for the release of all women *to* new life as well as *from* the present oppressive strictures, it has an important concomitant: the liberation of men from their own iron-clad role definitions which do not permit them to express emotion, to enjoy art, literature, music, or to engage in tasks like sewing, cooking, and child care without their "masculinity" being called into question. A culture which traps men in the rat race of competition for money, job, and sexual reputation is equally as oppressive of men as it is of women whom it coerces to be selfless in the most profound and devastating sense. The goal of the movement in this regard is a cultural affirmation of the best of both worlds: the integration within any individual *and* the larger society of the selfless and selfish aspects of human life so that all can achieve full personhood.

The present expressions of the women's liberation movement have as many forms as there are forms of oppression. A few examples are: the Media Women, who are concerned with the image of woman propagated by the mass media and with the employment of women in that field; Federally Employed Women, concerned with equal employment opportunities; the National Organization for Women, primarily professional women concerned with discrimination; and a variety of other groups, mostly of a radical political nature, such as Bread and Roses in Boston, Redstockings in New York, and others across the country called simply "Women's Liberation." Yet even with the vast spectrum of militancy and tactics represented, the groups have for the most part settled on major areas of agreement as to the principal immediate goals. We will merely enumerate them.

First, the provision of child-care facilities available to all women regardless of their employment, economic, or marital status. Such centers to be open twenty-four hours a day and staffed by both men and women who are qualified and enthusiastic about their work.

Second, the provision of courses in self-defense to enable all women to defend themselves against attack and coincidentally to keep women physically fit.

Third, the repeal of all abortion laws which do not allow a woman the right to the control of her own body.

Fourth, the revision of our history texts, courses, and so on, to include the contributions of women.

The Present Role of Women in the Church

Having examined the major directions of the women's liberation movement, let us turn now to a consideration of the image of woman projected by the church in its accumulated tradition. We must begin with a brief perusal of present denominational and local structures, for these necessarily reflect the institutional church's beliefs regarding women.

In local congregations, women are usually found in limited numbers on governing boards. Their responsibility is usually seen to be on Flower and Music committees, as Deaconess (an office which usually bears no real resemblance to that of Deacon) and Church School teacher. While women do comprise the large majority of active church members and are the sustaining force in almost every congregation, they have virtually no power within its structure, which is usually dominated by male clergy and church officers. As in the larger society, they are viewed as helpers for the men, with their only real talent seen to be in aesthetic matters or in working with children.

On the national staff of our denominations, it is almost impossible to find a woman executive outside the women's department. Occasionally we find a token woman in the Department of Christian Education, but even there she is a second-level executive. In the case of both staff and board or agency membership (denominational or ecumenical) the excuse often given is that clergy are needed in those positions, for they are the "leaders" of the church. Without even questioning the theology of ministry implicit in such a statement, one is still astounded at the view of woman represented there. Even those denominations which ordain women still do not consider them for higher positions. One major reason is that these women are located for the most part in small country churches which are not taken seriously by those in power. When they seek positions in city churches or in nonparochial situations, they are not given substantial support by their fellow clergy, seminaries, or national offices.

Thus it is apparent that the contemporary church's view of woman is that she is an aesthetically-minded, child-centered individual who has no talent for or interest in ordained ministry, administration, or policy-making positions.

The Tradition Behind the Role

Now let us examine our Christian theology and history to gain some clue as to what it is that has placed woman in her secondary position and has continued to reinforce that position for centuries. We will only briefly point to some of the most obvious questions to be raised. For a more profound and extensive analysis, the reader should consult Dr. Mary Daly's *The Church and the Second Sex* (Harper and Row, 1968).

The particular models which the church has lifted out of the Bible to represent women are invariably those of the temptress who leads man to his fall (Eve) or the unattainable ideal who combines both virginity and motherhood and who acquiesces at every turn to the male (Mary). In each of these cases, the church has chosen to emphasize certain parts of the biblical story and to ignore others. For instance, would not our image of woman differ radically from the present if the emphasis had been on either the creation story from Genesis 1 which affirms that "God created man in his own image . . . male and female he created them," or if Genesis 2, on the fact that by eating of the tree of the knowledge of good and evil, humanity was plunged into history rather than into sin *per se?*

Protestants have seldom taken a good look at the Virgin Mary as part of their heritage. For the most part, a fear of adulation has taken precedence over an interest in the imagery of woman. However, such a study is necessary, particularly at this juncture in history when women are becoming increasingly aware of their historical identity. There are many facets to Mary's personality and character, although the church has usually recognized only the simplest, that of a mother who adores her son. The theological possibilities inherent in taking Mary from the pedestal to which she has been chained and viewing her as a fully human, complex person are manifold. Luke indicates at several points that Mary was a profound, intelligent and assertive person. He relates her questioning her conception, her deep faith-response to that situation, and at least twice refers to her taking things to heart or pondering particular events. While we are told relatively little about Mary, that which we do know can hardly be interpreted as a woman who found her entire identity in the fact of her motherhood or in the person of her son. Indeed, she must be seen as a strong yet compassionate individual who was able to transcend her era's concept of woman as mother and homemaker. But the church has clung to its male-oriented understanding with a tenacity which can sometimes lead one to the conclusion that women should leave the present church structures and form their own church which would be more faithful to the true intent of Christ's life and teachings.

More attention should also be given to the fact that Jesus never made any explicit statement about women. Rather he demonstrated his attitude by his treatment of women like Mary Magdalene whose life of prostituting herself to men was transformed to a life of full personhood by her contact with Jesus and by his affirmation of her as a person. Theologians today who affirm that the New Testament must be examined in historical perspective and cultural context also affirm that in not urging women to take an active part with him, Jesus was facing the political realities of the day. The cultural blinders of first-century Palestine were such that the inclusion of women would probably have meant failure of his work. No competent theologian today takes the Pauline statements about women as prescriptive for the twentieth century.

Our theological language has clearly been developed by male theologians. One would be foolish to dispute the use of the masculine pronoun to refer to Jesus. Let it suffice to point out that his message, his style, his whole point was to open up life to people, in part by freeing them from "given," inescapable definitions and concepts of themselves. However, the use of the same pronoun to refer to God and to the Holy Spirit *must* be disputed. Even if we were to accept the convenient excuse that the language provides no alternative (recognizing that to opt for "she" would be as dehumanizing for men as "he" is for women), we must still question the "Father" image. One of the most valuable contributions to theology has been made by Christian Scientists: the concept of Mother-Father God. Yet, even this fails to solve our problems, however, as this symbol for the deity carries the restricting connotations our culture gives to mothers and fathers.

Historically, women have been disregarded, worshipped, or written off as fanatics with no great contribution to make to Christian life. Rather than attempt to scan two thousand years of history in a few pages, let us for a moment take a case in point: Anne Marbury

Hutchinson, who was born in England in 1590, banished from the Massachusetts Bay Colony in 1637, and died in what is now New York State in 1645. Historians have discredited Mrs. Hutchinson for over 300 years as a religiously fanatical woman who could not grasp the theological subtleties inherent in Puritan orthodoxy. Yet when we examine the primary sources (transcripts of her court and church trials, journals, correspondence), bearing in mind that all that is recorded came from her theological and political enemies, we are struck by the fact that historians have probably misunderstood her and her cause. A sympathetic reading of these sources sees her as a warm, intelligent, articulate person who was more understanding of her fellow colonists than the clergy, and who developed a theology capable of responding to their needs. She was no more religiously fanatical than anyone else of her time; indeed, in her ability to respond to people's needs and yet to stand within the Christian faith and tradition, it may be claimed that she was a greater Christian and lesser fanatic than any of her rigidly orthodox opponents.

This example can provide us with an insight into the treatment by historians of women in general or particular. It must be recognized, of course, that it is not merely church historians who have been guilty of this neglect and subjectivity. For instance, how many have heard of the Grimké sisters, Harriet Tubman, or Phoebe Palmer?

The Contemporary Church Perpetuates the Tradition

Turning to the church's involvement in the larger society, we note that the church presently, in subtle as well as direct ways, provides the underpinnings for the maintenance of the nuclear family system. In a time when social scientists are sharply aware of the fact that as presently structured the family cannot survive, one would expect the church to be seeking new directions for our life together. In point of fact, the church has seldom uttered a word of criticism directed at the family. One major cause of the breakdown of the family in America today is the way the family structure has exploited women. Society dictates that women are to fulfill themselves through husband and children, to give all of their time to their family without regard for themselves. They are to be married to the house and the work there. (What other meaning can the term *house-*

wife have?) And the church reinforces that mandate. Women everywhere have had to find their own ways to escape this situation. Divorce, alcoholism, and drugs are only some of the destructive symptoms of this deeply rooted malaise. The women's liberation movement seeks to join women together in the fight to end the suppression of women's creativity and consciousness.

The church understands its role in the community as a cementer of the family: "The family that prays together stays together." It is a marriage- and family-oriented institution. Christian Education programs are directed at children who come from whole families, yet a significant percentage of families are broken. Marriage counseling often results in continuation of marriages which are spiritually dead. Women are urged to adjust to their role as wives rather than attempt to forge a new life style for themselves. Institutionally, it is customary for few church women's meetings to be held in the evening when employed women can attend. When any church meeting is held, child care is seldom provided. As a matter of fact, their orientation is so directed at family, children, and the mythical "norm" that the single, divorced, or widowed woman finds little of interest to her.

It is indeed time for the church to come to grips with the way in which it supports societal institutions which oppress women. As we have indicated, a good hard look at the churches' hiring and buying patterns and the initiation of a program under Project Equality which would permit selective buying by the church could be an extremely effective weapon. The economic boycott of firms which discriminate against women would undoubtedly place the church in a hypocritical or embarrassing situation, for some denominations and ecumenical organizations would find that not only could they not purchase each other's goods or services, but in many cases they could not use their own!

And so we conclude that the status of woman in the church is no better than her status in the larger society. In both contexts, she is seen as servant to man (secretary, housekeeper, flower arranger, baby-sitter) and is assumed to have no other interests, talents or abilities. As we scan the culture, we become aware that the Judaeo-Christian heritage has in fact been one of the major causes of woman's present condition.

Women's Liberation and the Future of the Church

The conceptualization of woman as sex object which so pervades our media can be seen quite clearly to have had its earliest manifestation in Eve. So, too, the placing of woman on a pedestal can be seen to have had its early roots in man's understanding of Mary, the mother of Jesus. The organized church has theologically, politically, and economically supported social systems and institutions which greatly oppress women. It has done nothing to combat the rise of consumerism, the emphasis on the acquisition of things. Never has it spoken out about the degradation and exploitation of women in advertising. Little has been done to provide women encouragement and opportunities to find self-fulfillment in employment outside the home, and even less has been done to find new styles of living for families.

Many people are beginning to realize that the problems of our nation and the world will not be solved until we find the resources to deal with the issue of sexism, the myth of male supremacy. Not only has one-half of our population been denied the right and power to participate in our society, but in that deprivation, the life-giving values have also been denied. Our culture designates certain values, such as aggressiveness, competitiveness, and rationality, to the male, and others, such as compassion, co-operation, and nurture, to the female. Consequently, when one sex is excluded from participation, the values do not take root in the culture. Thus the present movement is an attempt to restore those neglected human values to their place. It is only through such restoration that humanity will be able to conquer the evils of war, racism, poverty, and pollution.

And, finally, it is only by the coming to consciousness of women in the church that there can be hope for the church's mission. It is not possible for the church to act with all its strength if more than half its membership is suppressed. Since women are the sustaining force in our churches, it is probable that the coming to consciousness of church women would result in the radicalizing of the church as a whole. If women were to recognize the ways in which both church and culture work together to limit their creativity and, indeed, their very life, they would rise up and confront clergy, retailers, deacons, insurance executives, and husbands every time they tried to say that God is a Father, that make-up is beautiful, that men's lives are worth more and are more important than women's.

If the church were to be radicalized—that is, returned to the fundamental ground of the Gospel, and to a critical stance against the institutions and false myths of the world—then it would find itself more alive and more at work than it has been since the Resurrection. We assert that the only means to accomplish this task is through the liberation of women and the setting free of those life-giving values which are chained to woman's pedestal.

Thus, church women throughout the world have a responsibility to work at this task, to begin with that institution closest to them, to radicalize it and to give it new life, and thereby change the very nature of the society in which we live, so that this can no longer be called a man's world.

WOMEN'S LIBERATION IN HISTORICAL AND THEOLOGICAL PERSPECTIVE*

by Rosemary Radford Ruether

The movement for women's liberation, which even in 1968 was scarcely on the agenda of the liberation movement in America, has now burst upon the scene like an angry Eve born from the Adam's rib of the New Left. In this present essay I would like to sketch something of the historical and theological background of the problem of the domination of women, particularly in Christian society. This background will also afford a context for viewing the theological significance of the movement of women's liberation as both a doctrine of humanity and a doctrine of the salvation appropriate to humanity that stands as a critique of classical Christian spirituality. The traditional dualism which women's liberation opposes may also give us some clues to the dialectic of liberation itself, the phases of development which a liberation movement goes through as it seeks maturity.

In order to discuss the liberation of women, we first have to understand the nature of the particular form of domination under which women suffer. It has been said that the domination of women is the most fundamental form of domination in society, and all other forms of domination, whether of race, class, or ethnic group draw upon the fantasies of sexual domination. This also suggests that the liberation of women is the most profound of all liberation movements, the most far-reaching revolution, because it gets to the roots of the impulse of domination. This does not necessarily mean that all women are necessarily worse off materially or more exploited, in the crudely physical sense of the word, than

* This article was prepared for the Winter 1970 issue of *Soundings:* An Interdisciplinary Journal.

other groups, but rather that the fundamental meaning of human alienation and the subjection of one person to another, as well as the overcoming of alienation in true reciprocity and communication, finds its most fundamental existential expression here, although it may be expressed in cruder and more obvious form in relation to racial or class exploitation.

In an article which I published on this subject in *Cross Currents* two years ago,[1] I suggested that the domination of women is rooted in the fundamental schism and alienation in the male psyche that emerged in the course of the evolution of the mind as a self-conscious and reflective ego. In pre-literate tribal societies, the reflective self-consciousness is still submerged in the collective mind of the community. Women and men have their respective roles and religious cults within it. Women too have their mysteries where they are priestesses and represent the divine principle as Mother goddess, from which men are excluded, as women are excluded from the mysteries of male initiation. The relationship is not one of rivalry, nor does it seem that the evidences of female religious and social authority in early societies are correctly to be called "matriarchy" as some anthropologists have thought, for here there is no more reversal of later patriarchal domination. Rather both sexes have their roles within the overarching myth of the world which encompasses them both.

Domination and the Ego

The emergence of male domination, I postulated, coincides with the emergence of the self-conscious, individualized ego, which now objectifies the world and conceives of itself as standing over against the world as the object of its manipulation and control. There may be more than just economic truth to the Marxist theory that the domination of women arises with the advent of private property. Both would express the more primal alienation of man from nature. Nature no longer encompasses man as a common mother, but is set apart from his person as property to be divided up and possessed in private parcels. Along with his land, his slaves, and his cattle, his women now become a part of man's private property, to be bartered and used accordingly. The triumphant ego, which has emerged from nature, begins to conceive of itself as totally independent from nature, as an alien and lonely species which has dropped to this earthly sphere from a different and invisible world, and which can maintain its own freedom and integrity only by sharply differentiating itself from all that pertains to the outward world. This sharp dualism of the rational ego and the outward world comes to full expression in Greek civilization. Plato's myth of the soul as a spiritual being which sojourns in the body as an alien in a lower world, is its primary myth of the logos as a self-subsistent reality. This myth of the soul expressed itself both in body-soul dualism and in male-female dualism. In fact, the two are interdependent expressions of the same alienation. The logos in Greek civilization is essentially male. In Plato's creation myth, the *Timaeus,* the soul is put into the body as a testing place. If it lives righteously, it will return to its native star. But if it succumbs to the body, it will pass into the form of a woman at its second birth, and from thence into the body of some brute which resembles the evil nature which it has acquired, until finally by ascetic purification and contemplative ascent it wins its way back to manhood and raises itself to the philosophical life which will finally free it of the trammels of matter.[2] This same view is adopted by the Fathers of the Church, who, following Philo's Platonist interpretation of the Genesis creation story, teach that God created an original archetypal spiritual humanity, and the advent of bodiliness, femaleness, and sexuality occurs only as a result of the Fall.[3] In Gregory of Nyssa's treatise *On the Creation of Man,* Augustine's commentary *On Genesis against the Manichaeans* and other Patristic commentaries on Genesis, the creation of woman is regularly linked with the fall of the original spiritual principle of man into bodiliness and sin.

Dualism in Classical Thought

In this tradition it is hard to disentangle anti-female prejudice from anti-bodily prejudice, for the two intermingle. The soul, or more specifically, its rational component, is man's authentic nature. The body in Greek thought was defined as the prison house of the soul, distorting and bestializing it and fettering it to the earth. The body was the seat of the lower, antagonistic self from which man must struggle to free himself in order to be saved. Salvation from the body was the primary expression of the salvation myth in this Greek tradition, and, as such, was incorporated into and deeply molded classical Christian spirituality, all but submerging the original Biblical eschatology of the resurrection of the body. This meant that, despite many elements in the Christian tradition that told against it, woman was set to be cast in the role of the very incarnation of sin, the flesh, and the world. This view is unleashed without reservation in some passages of the monastic writers especially. Even where it is kept in check by contrary traditions in the main stream of Christian theology, the basic prejudice is expressed in the ambiguous treatment of women which, while accepting elements of humanity and capacity for salvation in her, nevertheless treats her as dangerous, tempting man toward his lower self, more given to carnal desires and less capable of rational restraint than man.

I have suggested that the root of this deep-seated dualism in classical Western thought lies in an alienation within the human psyche, expressed by the emergent male as the originator of this dualism. In modern psychoanalysis the consciousness or ego is seen as a small island or promontory thrust up from the waters of the total psyche. The evolutionary innovation of reflective individuality and self-consciousness was expressed by standing in an antagonistic relation to the larger psyche. The unconscious becomes a dark, threatening enemy which would engulf it and from which it must struggle to separate itself in order to be itself. This basic antagonism which emerges within the psyche is projected in the subject-object dualism. Objective, somatic reality is invested with the images of the lower self. The body and indeed outer visible reality as such is seen as the antagonist of the conscious self and the source and expression of temptations and delusions which threaten to submerge the mind. This same dualism is also projected sociologically, the woman being cast in the role of the lower self. The witch, the maenad who follows in the train of Dionysus, the devouring Earth Mother represent the frightening images of suppressed psychic powers. The fantasies of sexual projection are also invested in other objects of sociological domination as well. Class, race, and ethnic domination tends to project a very similar stereotype on the suppressed group, and whether it be Negro, peasant-proletariat, oriental, or Jewish, it takes on the images of the lower self. He is fickle, bestial, passionate, yet at the same time passive, irrational, contemptible; dangerous, fundamentally lacking in the qualities of reason that define full humanity.

In order to understand the sociological workings of psychic projection, we must see the way the projection tends to be internalized by the subjugated group. The projected images dictate the social role they are allowed to play. This in turn molds their own self-image so that they largely take on the appearance, not only in the presence of the oppressors, but even in their own eyes, of the character vested in them. This is reinforced by exclusion from educational and vocational opportunities for corrective and enlarging experiences. The subjugated group is not allowed to experience itself in any way except through the image and role which the dominant society has cut out for it. Also, its psychology is restricted to a one-sided development, and so the social myth of fixed, inherited natures acts as a self-fulfilling prophecy. Social dualism of this character seems to be typical of classical Western civilization. Nor can we find a great difference here between its classical and its Christian periods, since Christian civilization so largely appropriated the cultural character of classical civilization.

Dualism Today

This synthesis of classical and Christian civilization has been going through a massive upheaval, dissolution, or transformation in the last few hundred years, from the Renaissance to the Enlightenment and the French Revolution, to the wars and cultural revolutionary struggles of our own day. Certainly one characteristic of this period of continual revolutions has been a struggle to overcome all these forms of social domination and the dualistic supporting ideologies inherited from traditional society. Class, racial, sexual, and, perhaps we should add, generational alienations come out in the open. Characteristic of this revolutionary struggle is the repudiation of the classical salvation myth of the flight of the soul from the woman, the body, and the world, and the embrace of a new salvation myth that looks to the reintegration of humanity in a new community through the overthrow of domination and alienation. The vision of a reintegrated community of humanity in a new communion with nature runs through the future hopes of all the social struggles of the last two centuries. Karl Marx in his early explorations of alienation in the *Economic-Philosophical Manuscripts* describes the birth of the new communist order in these words:

Communism is the positive abolition of private property, of human self-alienation, and thus is the real appropriation of human nature through and for man. It is, therefore, the return of man to himself as a social, i.e. really human being, a complete and conscious return which assimilates all the wealth of the previous development. Communism as a fully developed naturalism is humanism and as a fully developed humanism is naturalism. It is the definitive resolution of the antagonism between man and nature and between man and man. It is the true solution of the conflict between existence and essence, between objectification and self-affirmation, between freedom and necessity, between individual and species. It is the solution of the riddle of history. . . . Only then is nature the basis of his own human experience and a vital element of human reality. The natural existence of man has here become his human existence and nature itself has become human for him. [Communist] society is the accomplished union of man with nature, the veritable resurrection of nature, the realized naturalism of man and the realized humanism of nature.[4]

In an interview published in his *Post-Prison Speeches and Writings,* Eldridge Cleaver also speaks of the new society for which he is working as one where man will be reintegrated with himself, with other men, and with his own body. The overcoming of racial oppression will bring a reintegration of the white man with his body and a reintegration of the black man with his intellect. This reunion of each race with the submerged and projected parts of their own natures will also be found to be a reconciliation of male and female.

Only when people, black and white, start seeing themselves and acting as total individuals, with minds and bodies, will they stop assigning mental roles to one set of people and exclusively physical roles to another. Only then will the primary thrust of life, the fusion of male and female, be freed of sociological obstacles.[5]

But this reunion of man with his total social and cosmic body is a vision which still eludes post-classical, post-Christian man. Nature grows, if anything, more alienated from us and shows ever more the distorting marks of man's rapacity. Social alienation within societies and between nations around the world grows sharper. Man now seems to be on the brink of an apocalyptic alternative. The new communal society becomes no longer an over-optimistic dream. More and more it appears as the practical necessity for averting the holocaust that can annihilate the world, for the fiery apocalypse, too, has now become a practical possibility.

In Albert Camus' classic book *The Rebel,* rebellion is shown to be the affirmation of a common humanity as the ground upon which the rebel protests his own dehumanization. Rebellion is communication; the breaking of silence between oppressed and oppressor. This is the beginning of humanization. The revolt is not merely against external conditions, but ultimately against the way in which oppression has crept into and distorted one's own soul. Of all rebellious groups the blacks have been perhaps the most acute in recognizing the internal workings of prejudice and understanding rebellion as a cultural-psychological exorcism of oneself in a remaking of one's own identity and self-image. Here is an area where the black experience, it seems to me, still has much to teach women.

Various social barriers still hold woman back from exploring her full capacities, but the chief form of enslavement of women is psychological and cultural. The cultural projection of acceptable feminine images and woman's internalization of these limited views of her identity and potential is the primary tool which keeps sexual domination intact. Woman's chief enemy is herself—or rather her own internalization of these limiting images. It is also on this psychological-cultural level that women are most vulnerable to ridicule and shame and least able to sort out their discontent. The chief act of rebellion for a woman, then, is an internal one; a grasping of a confident faith in her own full personhood and a rejection of servitude to self-images which dry up her creative expansion. This inner rebellion is never unrelated to the objective forces which project and enforce the demeaning image, however. Humanity is mysteriously social in its being, and we can seldom possess our souls in isolation from the way we are known by society. It seems to me impossible to be fully content in one's own self-knowledge when this conflicts with society's image of one. Consequently inner rebellion extends itself into the social sphere as cultural revolution to reshape the social currency of values. That we can rise above and break the chains of the social image is an expression of the transcendent dimension of humanity, but we are also immanent in it to the degree that we cannot be at peace with ourselves until we remold culture to reflect this fuller self-knowledge. No psychic revolution can really be complete without its accompanying social revolution.

Struggle Against Cultural Oppression

Cultural revolutionary struggle, it seems to me tends to go through several complementary phases in its efforts to overthrow the wiles of the enemy. These different stages both reflect a correct discernment of aspects of the cultural oppression by the dominant society, and are nonetheless controlled, by way of reaction, by the projected images of the dominant society. The breakthrough to full humanity and community still eludes the rebel.

The first stage might be described as one of emulation of the dominant society. The oppressed seeks to win his place by being as much like the oppressor as possible. One finds this in the early feminist movements in the late nineteenth and early twentieth centuries. Women sought to emerge by beating men at their own game of rational, aggressive, manipulative logos. The noted Eastern women's colleges were founded on the assumption that women should prove that they were capable of a "man's education," which, at that time, was largely the classical-humanistic curriculum. By proficiency in Greek, Latin, logic, philosophy, history and science, not to mention sports, women would prove their equality with men.[6] Women won their rights to new vocations in business and politics by showing that they were capable of the same cool, impersonal reason that was presumed essential to the "man's world." Early feminists were often masculine in dress, and some even culminated their struggle with a vision of a new homosexual society of masculinized women, in which the male sex had become superfluous. In the very style of this type of rebellion we can see women's symbiotic interaction with male prejudice. Women saw their liberation by way of hating and repudiating all that had been marked off as essentially feminine, especially the female role in marriage and childbearing. Moreover, males also accepted this masculinized female in a controlled form, as the basis for allowing women into new social roles. The new women who were allowed to type in offices or work in factories must not look too feminine. They could look a little pert, but in a sterilized way that would not interfere with their efficiency. Socialist societies took over this stage of the feminist rebellion and appropriated the masculinized woman who could be dressed in the same baggy pants as the male worker and put to work beside him in the same factory job.

In reaction against the distortions of this stage of the rebellion we saw in the nineteen-forties a rush of women back to the home and childbearing to recover dimensions of their being which their crusading mothers had seemed too willing to sacrifice. Women in this period in America retreated from many of the vocational advances that they had made and re-embraced with new fervor the traditional roles which society had assigned to them. Betty Friedan's book *The Feminine Mystique* well recorded the neuroticisms of this apparently newly contented housewife. But this period does not seem to me to be all loss. Women instinctively recognized that liberation based on self-hatred was simply a capitulation to another side of the enslavement. Liberation proceeds dialectically, as enslavement itself is dialetctical.

One can see a similar dialectic in the black liberation movement. Blacks first sought to win their place by being as much like the white man as possible, submerging everything that characterized them as Negroes, culturally and physically. Having proved to themselves their capacity for the white man's games, they then began to reject the alienation and loss of their own "soul." The next stage of the rebellion was a conscious embracing of everything black and the flowering of a new black cultural identity. Although this movement often takes the ghetto black as a cultural hero, in point of fact the leaders of this movement of black cultural rebellion are generally sons of the black middle class, the sons of that very class of Negroes who, in an earlier generation, had vindicated their ability to emulate the style and skills of the white man.

Harking Back to Past

However the black man, by the very nature of his oppression, could find no salvation in a mere embrace of traditional black identity, for this ultimately was the identity of a slave. His self-assertion must be the creation of a new blackness which had never before been seen in this land; a powerful, exultant, lithe and beautiful blackness which attacked the white stereotype at its roots. Such probing could scarcely avoid, at some point, acting out the white man's most fearsome images of the black man as the ultimate defiance. The "Black Panther" ready to pounce on "whitey," perhaps rape his woman (but never marry her); the black man in triumphant virility, poised with a large machine gun in his hands; this was a black man probing the underbelly of fear and hatred; a necessary phase, I believe, but still one molded by reaction and not the goal of mature self-knowledge.

In a similar way some of the radical groups of the new women's liberation movement act out the underside of male dread of unleashed feminine power. Ancient images again rise from the earth in the Magna Mater style adopted by some of the hippy women. The women of the protest movements are maenads with wild tossing locks, all social mores cast aside. Even the image of the witch, the fearsome woman who stands at the crossroads in the dark of the moon, leaps up to confront the dominant society. This apotheosis of unleashed feminine power was celebrated in the recent living theatre productions of the *Bacchae* and *Dionysus '69* where the bacchantes, with bloodied hands, triumphantly hold up the severed head of Pentheus, the king-priest of society. In the same way, it should not surprise us that one of the most militant of the women's liberation groups has chosen to call itself WITCH (Women's International Terrorist Conspiracy from Hell) and to act out their confrontation with black pointed hats and chanted curses.

In and through these various social interactions with oppression, however, I believe that all the rebellious groups in post-classical, post-Christian society are seeking a new communal personhood whereby all people recover and reintegrate into their soul those aspects of life which they previously denied to themselves or denied others. Each person seeks his full soul, and more and more we discover that this cannot be done without the resurrection of all humanity together, for each group has shared in the alienation, and so there can be no salvation for one which is not the salvation of all. It seems to me that it is not difficult for someone with a Biblical culture to recognize the affinity of this new social aspiration with the Biblical hope for the Kingdom of God. Unlike the classical salvation myth of the flight of the soul, the Biblical salvation myth is one of reintegration of man in community and nature in a total apotheosis of all creation. In Marx's words, "It is the solution of the riddle of history," where all the paradoxes of man—individual and community, man and nature, body and spirit, finitude and infinity—come together in mutual transformation. In other words, the salvation myth of post-classical man is far closer to the Biblical hope than the classical view. However, the irony of this situation vis à vis classical Christian civilization is that Christian culture took over and absorbed the classical view of man and its myth of salvation, and so molded its social institutions accordingly that it now finds itself the foe of the new culture-bearers of its own original tradition. This is nowhere more true than in the social structure and culture of that group which is most closely associated with the church: the clergy. They appear as almost the last bastion of the "old humanity" where anti-feminine, anti-bodily patriarchalism still reigns. This means that the church can only recover its own original gospel of the New Creation of the resurrected body by dying to a culture and social structure with which it has most deeply identified itself. This also means that the avant garde of the "new humanity" have lost their own roots in finding it all but impossible to recognize the Christian Church as anything but the oldest and most entrenched of their foes.

NOTES

1. "The Becoming of Women in Church and Society," *Cross Currents*, 17 (Fall 1967), 418–426.
2. *Timaeus*, 42.
3. Philo, *De opificio mundi;* the same view is repeated in such patristic commentaries on Genesis as Gregory of Nyssa's *De opificio hominis* and Augustine's *De Genesi contra Manichaeos*.
4. "Private Property and Communism," *Economic-Philosophical Manuscripts*, ed. Fromm, p. 127.
5. (Random House, 1968), pp. 206–209.
6. See my article "Are Women's Colleges Obsolete?" *Critic* (Oct.–Nov., 1968), pp. 58–64.

A CHRISTIAN PERSPECTIVE ON FEMINISM

by Sidney Cornelia Callahan

"How can you be a feminist and a Christian at the same time? And a Catholic, at that? Besides, you are happily married and have *six* children!"

"Yes," I reply, "all those statements are true, but there is not as much conflict as you might suppose between radical Christianity and radical feminism."

Once launched into such a dialogue, I can say with all honesty that my conversion to Christianity preceded my feminism . . . and aided and abetted it. Without taking Christianity seriously I would never have been prepared to accept radical feminism. My arguments with feminism also spring from Christian sources, but I'll get to that later.

First and foremost, serious Christianity taught me to reappraise the world I knew with a different eye. As a Christian I could no longer accept the passing scene with a shrug and, "Well, that's just the way things are." I became critical of everything, because I measured everything by Christ's words in the Gospel and the rest of the New Testament. The value of each individual whom God loved was not to be ignored, suppressed, harmed in any way. Prejudice against women seemed as offensive to God as prejudice against blacks or the poor or Jews. In other words the wrongs against women were just one more example of things that had to be righted in the name of justice.

I also got the very clear message that the responsibility for bringing the kingdom of God to earth was mine. No excuse of weakness or anything else was accepted. It never occurred to me that because I was a woman I could excuse myself from the tasks to be done. After all, there were the women saints to look to; and since God worked through weakness (according to St. Paul), what did it matter that I didn't belong to the dominant caste, or sex. My aspiration was to serve and love and change the world, and femininity didn't seem to be something that would get in the way.

I was also saved from what the radical feminists call passive sexism, in which women aim only to please other people, particularly if they are men. In serious Christianity the point was to get beyond appearances and the desire to exercise power over others. As a woman I wanted to look nice, but pleasing men was not as important as pleasing God by right actions. What's inside the head is far more important. Depth of personality and intelligence were more valuable than popularity. It was wrong and self-indulgent to get too self-conscious and self-involved. Christianity forced me to give up female narcissism and timidity, as much as I could manage, anyway. My aim was to make something of myself, not to make it with men.

Growing Up a Christian

At the same time, I guess, I was helped by being the eldest in a two-girl family, going to an all-girls school, and attending an all-girls bluestocking college. My parents expected the highest achievements from me and so did my teachers and professors. In the world I lived in I never met failure or prejudice because I was a girl. I just remember being deeply happy that I was feminine and capable of childbirth as well as everything else. Used to success, it never occurred to me that being a woman was a handicap.

All my attention was focused on functioning as a Christian in a worldly world. Here is where I felt prejudice and tension. Here, too, is where I was to develop discipline and toughness. In secular society during the '50s, especially in intellectual academic circles, Christianity was considered an unacceptable ideology. One got used to being considered "queer," "odd," "different," "fanatic," and so on. I learned early the effort required to go against the crowd, even those I most admired, and stick to my unpopular beliefs.

As a serious Christian I also held very different ideas about sexual conduct than most of my peers. Most girls were not as strict as I was (this was before the full development of the sexual revolution) and most boys were saddened over my misguided standards. Never mind. If men wanted to take me out, and they did, they conformed to my standards. Happily, I had a wonderful, idyllic time, went everywhere, made lots of friends, and never, never felt sexually exploited. An early marriage to a fellow idealist and intellectual Christian protected me from cynicism about men. Marrying young and well while still in college kept me from facing all those problems of sexual and economic exploitation that can bedevil young single women in the world alone.

By working very hard, I managed to finish college before our first baby was born. A greater triumph lay in being able to beat the male obstetrical establishment by having my baby without medicine or stitches. Glorious ecstatic experience! Nursing was also nice, and my husband and I cared for the baby alone, alike in our ignorance and dependence on Dr. Spock. We were determined to share our family life, our intellectual life and everything else in a loving and equal way. But I was also determined to master cooking and house-keeping, which had been mysteries to me before marriage. "Oh, when the big bubbles come, that means the water is boiling . . . right?" Manual labor and the domestic arts seemed like real life, after sixteen years of studying, studying, studying.

So at the beginning of our graduate student life, I reveled in battling poverty, mastering the motherly arts, and reading all the things I had never got around to in college. It was an education in reality which was invaluable for a middle-class child. I found I could take it. Four babies all under age four in four rooms with no money is a real challenge! My husband, for his part, was battling the grim graduate school grind and we were both incredibly toughened by our ascetic life.

Gradually, however, I began to become embittered at the discrepancy between the male and female roles society was forcing upon us. My intellectual talents had no encouragement or chance for expression. I was snowed under by repetitive physical labor, with no part-time graduate school available, no child-care facilities, no fellowships for married women, no part-time work. My husband's life was miserable too, but he was able to choose a career *and* have the joy of family life. Economic and social necessity forced us to divide our lives, assume very different functions and become unequal members of society.

Since I had no formal status as a student and could not manage to study as much or get a degree, I became in the eyes of the world mostly my husband's wife and my children's mother. As we struggled out of the academic slums and into suburbia, my misery increased. No more intellectual friends were around to talk to about things I read. My husband was far away in the city. We weren't poor enough any more to make housekeeping a monumental struggle to survive. But we weren't rich enough yet to hire good helpers and afford graduate school. I was bored, frustrated and confused over my feminine role.

My conflict was intensified because my Christianity held up the ideal of self-sacrifice and service for the sake of love. Why could I no longer love enough to give up intellectual pursuits and intellectual work? The upheaval and inner questioning caused me suffering of a new kind. Out of that agony I was finally able to come to some decisions. I decided there was a fine line between sacrifice and suicide. I could not live without intellectual function and some systematic nondomestic work in the adult world. To try to live the traditional feminine role would be suicide and a betrayal as well of the ideals and equality of our marriage. Ten years without formal intellectual work or study was all that I could bear. During those years I had helped launch my husband and created a family and functioning household. Now I had to put myself first for a while or sink.

My personal solution was mostly due to luck. I began to write and gradually got enough money to go back to graduate school. The return to a structured intellectual world of work and school was an ecstatic experience. My reading and study was now focused and more efficient, since it was not solitary. New adult vistas opened for me, new competencies were discovered. My despair over a repetitive unstimulating work week disappeared. Life seemed full of zest again as I resumed the identity and work which was too much at the core of my personality to deny. I could never go back to a life without work and an independent adult function in society separate from family. I still have many, many conflicts and problems in combining work and family life, but they are better conflicts than my old self-destructive embittered conflicts born of frustration and boredom. I chose them freely.

Overcoming the "Feminine Mystique"

Here, too, the feminists are right. Women need to have the right to choose. Self-determination and responsibility for how one will spend one's talents and energy are essential. For many educated women it's not enough to concentrate only on one husband, one family, and one household. They need interaction with a larger community and the ongoing work of the world. When the work of the world and the children and men shift from the home, women naturally want to follow. In this way, Christian ideals of commitment to the community and neighbors beyond family can be expressed as well. Interaction with others doesn't have to be professional or consist of paid work, but as an adult one needs other adults and a community in order to keep growing and to keep from stagnating in isolation. Men are forced through economic necessity and their expected roles in society to keep moving, meet new people, master new challenges and keep getting involved.

Women, who have the same needs as men in this respect, must make greater efforts to counter the culture's pressure to keep them as passive dependent consumers. A strong personality must learn to plan and focus activity rather than drift through life and dissipate talents. Women all too often are not encouraged to make life plans or consider the future. They are encouraged to live only in the present, to be concerned only with expression rather than action, and to be complementary to some man's life, rather than to live their own. Yet one's identity depends on carrying out purposes in time and being responsible for one's self.

I believe Christianity also encourages women to develop more initiative and responsibility. Older ideas about Eve and woman's place as subordinate give way before better theology and biblical scholarship. (This I tried to show in my book, *The Illusion of Eve*.) Women, like men, are told to become sons of God, growing into Christ. After all, God is not male or female, or male and female, but uniquely divine. Both men and women are to be bride and son in the Christian community. This means, I think, that they are both to develop creative receptivity *and* aggressive initiative and responsibility. In Catholicism Mary's importance can be seen as an explicit revocation of the curses of Genesis. No more feminine subordination to husbands. No more pain in childbirth. No more nonsense about women being unclean and so unfit for the priesthood. The free "Yes" of Mary affirms her role as the daughter of Israel, the innovator and trusted creature initiating justice. The Magnificat is a proud searing song, having nothing to do with passivity, sweetness, timidity, or the feminine mystique.

Alas, the so-called feminine mystique has been entrenched in Christian thought. Despite the example of saints like Joan of Arc and Teresa of Avila, women have been told to be passive and docile. The overemphasis upon sexuality was partly to blame. Sex was seen to be a lot more important, and dangerous, than it really is. This shouldn't be the case in a community which affirms celibacy. Christian celibacy quite explicitly affirms that a person is a person first and not just an appendage to sexual function. Sex is made for man and not man for sex. The celibate vocation has always affirmed that men and women are masters of their sexuality. It is ironic that radical women's liberation groups also often espouse celibacy in order to free women from their cultural definition as sexual objects. Women must be redefined as persons in themselves, not in relation to men or children. This is also the precondition for good marriages.

New Life Styles for Women

Now, when such happily married women begin to resume full adult social identity they do have many problems and conflicts, as I mentioned above. The best of men, who want complete equality in their marriages, have difficulty putting their ideals into practice. The culture does not expect men to work at being equal, and often men have to take a lot of criticism from other men if they do housework or help with the children. It's hard for members of a dominant group to give up their privileges, or relinquish the feeling that they are bestowing favors rather than granting rights. Most men are under competitive pressures in their work, and under financial strains. More demands from home will at times seem onerous. Worse still, the competitive culture keeps pushing men and women, husbands and wives, into competitive stances. People compare and criticize capacities and achievements. The couple involved has to really work at co-operating rather than competing.

A threatened man can make life very difficult for his wife in a period of transition. He can criticize, demand more, and say that his wife is ignoring him and the children. Often such a man doesn't even realize that he is creating problems. He just feels vaguely hurt that his wife is not satisfied in her identity as wife and mother. *He* could not be just husband and father but he keeps thinking or hoping that with women it's different. All too often it is different; women are so vulnerable to criticism that they need strength and support to go in new directions. Here Christians gain strength from prayer and the effort to submit themselves to the judgment of God rather than men. A women's group which can give support is also a great help. Those husbands who find their newly stimulated wives more stimulating can also give reassurance to both husband and wife in transition.

For most women, however, the main conflict over re-entry into society will come because of the needs of their children. We know how tremendously much care and stimulation children need. Ironically, there are now fewer workers available for child care, since it has not been a high prestige job. Yet, at the same time, women not only enjoy caring for their children more than ever before, but they have been led to believe that it is imperative they be on the job every moment. Since this has been society's viewpoint, women who wanted to work or who had to work felt guilty and often were severely criticized by others.

It now appears from further research into personality formation, that the over-all influences of the family configuration are more important than the mother's constant presence. The personalities of all involved, the relationship of the parents, the status and values of the family as a whole, and the quality of the substitute care that the child receives are important. Yes, babies need continuing constant caretakers who love them; but they seem able to adjust to several important figures in their life rather than a one and only mothering figure.

Since most women will no longer have huge families they can look forward to relatively few years of intense child care and will choose to make the most of them. Women do not like to miss too much of their children's development. Since there are still few child-care facilities or child-care workers, most women will not work before their children go to school. Even then, part-time work is the perfect solution while family obligations are still heavy. Time for leisure and just playing is necessary for every family. If things get too hectic, scheduled and strained, everybody suffers.

Perhaps the most perfect life style emerging is that of the lucky parents who can both work less than a full week, or work at their own discretion at home. In this situation both parents can participate in the lives of the children and both can work among adults in the community. A full sharing of roles plus time for leisure as a family is ideal. Men can cultivate their creative nurturing qualities just as women can develop more aggression and competency. Children benefit from sharing in the lives of their parents. They should not always be segregated and pushed off with their peers. Men, women and children do best when they can live together and enjoy one another in a common life.

Husbands and children should not really be seen as "the work" of a woman. You don't mold a person or work on him as you do on a project or impersonal task. Child rearing is a human relationship, a mutual sharing of human potential, which is best done in some bigger context. Adults are too aggressive and high-powered to center totally on a child's upbringing, which is slow and depends more on the activity of the child rather than the adult. I, for one, am a much better mother when my work is absorbing lots of energy and I am able to live *with* my children rather than work on them. Family life can remain low-keyed and relaxed when it's not my sole justification for living. My work gives my children growing room and space to breathe.

Work has helped me to live up to my Christian conviction that my children are free to choose and to act. They must live their own lives; I can't live them for them. Somehow I was so eager to be a good mother that I could not allow them their own guilt or freedom to err. Their mistakes were really my mistakes. It was hard for me to let them go and see them as separate persons who had to act on their own to grow up. I tend to smother them and spoil them when I don't have a life of my own.

However, things are so complicated that the other danger is always present too. We, as parents, can get so wrapped up in our own lives that we don't pay just the right amount of attention to someone who needs at that moment to be pressured or pampered. Women, like their husbands, always have to be on guard that they don't get too engrossed in their absorbing adult world and start lowering their standards of parental care. I think after the first heated excitement of re-entry into the adult world of work has cooled down women can gauge the amount of work that they can take on without straining their family life. Men often do not have this choice, but even they have to face some such decisions and consider the whole family in their career choices. The old work ethic of putting achievement before people is increasingly questioned and rejected by many Americans, particularly the young; the Christian ideal of putting people first has begun to penetrate the culture.

A Christian Approach to Liberation

At just this juncture and over the question of the primacy of people, there seems to be a split in the feminist movement. At this point my Christianity and my feminism often begin to conflict. I too want to see women liberated. I want to see women leaders in politics, in the professions, women priests, ministers, bishops, women artists. However, I don't want women to ape the most offensive characteristics of the western male. How can women liberate themselves and their sisters without resorting to violence, aggressiveness, competitiveness and enmity toward men as their oppressors?

My answer follows the model of Christ, Gandhi, Martin Luther King and not that of the radical revolutionaries. I think love and education, soul force and truth force are the only means which will work in the long run. Loving one's enemies and oppressors keeps one from imitating them and falling into their same errors. We want women to become aggressive in the good sense, not in the destructively aggressive way that men have adapted. Besides, it takes more strength to be peaceful; you can't keep turning your own inadequacies into aggression against some enemy out there. Love and peacefulness keep you plugging away on your own course without distraction; it also keeps you flexible enough to be creative and surprising in your tactics. Without blinding hate you can take advantage of any new possibilities that come your way. You can also see things from the other person's point of view and show him how it's to his advantage to come to an agreement.

Women, like blacks, want to be free to make their own contributions in any area of American life that they may choose, and the culture would benefit from their increased participation. Men and women may be more alike than different, but cultural conditioning has made women warmer, more person-centered and sensitive to the preservation of life. The culture at large needs these qualities badly. I would like to see a woman's liberation movement which by liberating women could produce the liberation of people in general. Loving a husband and having five sons, I see the need for men to be freed from the terrible aspects of the male role. I hope the rise of women can signal the rise of co-operative communal models of human interaction rather than competitive, individualistic, aggressive ways of running a society.

While women need to have more of the traditionally masculine qualities of independence and initiative, the culture as a whole needs to be more "feminine." I see this as synonymous with saying that the culture needs to be more open to Christian values. In a sense my major conflict with radical feminism turns on this affirmation that the traditional feminine qualities of love and care are the basic realities of the universe. Faith in a God of Love keeps me from fighting, hating or destroying in order to gain ascendancy.

Also, I cannot look upon nature and the body and its processes as completely neutral. Belief in a Creator and a final purpose entails for me the belief that man must respect nature and subdue it . . . not destroy or remake it. Women who proclaim their right to control their bodies seem to make of the body a machine disconnected from themselves, and from the human species. They also ignore the involuntary processes of life which sustain us every moment of every day. Freedom of the will also means accepting processes, not just being able to reverse a process. Mechanical and chemical contraception seems to me a way to subdue fertility for human ends, but a way to control fertility without drastic intervention in bodily processes would be preferable. Some way to co-operate with the body as a mother does following the psychoprophylatic method of childbirth would be more satisfactory. The control of childbearing through abortion also seems a most horrible negation of life and love. The feminist cry for abortion on demand is a throwback to an individualistic freedom-of-my-private-property concept of human life. It's difficult to see this as progress toward communal and co-operative models of life and life-giving growth. Freedom is not an ultimate value justifying everything.

I guess in the end my feminism must be finally subordinated to the demands of Christian faith. Women's liberation is also not an ultimate value or a cause overriding all others. For me, radical feminism must also be put into a larger context and a longer race. But while radical Christianity and radical feminism share the same course they do move each other along. Or so I have found.

EDUCATION FOR LIBERATION: WOMEN IN THE SEMINARY

by Susan Copenhaver Barrabee

I must begin by saying that at this point in my life I have decided to make only occasional attempts to seem terribly objective on the subject of women anywhere, and women in the seminary will be no exception. This is not because I feel it is pointless to struggle against my "God-given nature" (*i.e.,* emotional, intuitive, unconscious, illogical, etc.); neither is it because I cannot reason. Rather it is because I feel that most people have very strong biases on subjects dealing with sexual identity and I do not think it possible for most men and women in our culture to speak with any significant detachment about things concerning their own sexual roles. I think there would be a great deal more clarity on such subjects if more "authorities" and "mature" (or at least so they are considered on other matters) thinkers could somehow bring themselves to deal openly with the mire of deeply conditioned responses in which we are all caught when it comes to the question of male and female and how they function in our society.

The Seminary Experience

Seminaries are institutions of higher learning which define themselves as places in which theological education takes place. This has traditionally meant that the professional leadership (the clergy) for the church (the body and bride of Christ) is trained and pronounced ready to be invested as minister, pastor, rector, priest, and so on. It has also meant that the seminary has been the center for serious theological reflection.

Today many seminaries are engaging in very broadly defined theological reflection and are in significant dialogue with other academic disciplines as well as with contemporary culture. Seminaries today are producing large numbers of graduates who see their ministries in a radically new light and who have very tenuous, if any, ties to the traditional work of the church in its highly institutionalized forms. Many graduates who take places of leadership in the institutional church itself are determined that its place in society is not simply to rubber-stamp the direction already established in the order of things but to work out new directions no matter how threatening the process might become.

I make the latter observations because I am not unaware of the meaningful steps being taken in the circles of theological education to move into the twenty-first century without allowing tradition to function as blinders. I am excited enough by the possibilities of theological education that I would rather be in a seminary now than anywhere else. Having said all that and having meant it, I nevertheless am compelled to say that from the point of view of women increasingly committed to change in the image and function of woman in this society, a look at the seminary yields a *very* dismal picture.

I have never been involved with an institution in which I was more aware of being female. I am definitely out of my "place" as a student in a theological school. I think that I was supposed to get the message even before I got here. The medium is undeniably male. The main characters of Christian theology: God, a father; Christ, his son; the Holy Spirit, an impregnator, among other more elusive things; and Man (as in "the nature of"), although purported to be a generic designation, are unmistakably male. The Bible and all of the great theological tomes over which we pore have been penned by men. Seminary professors and clergy are almost without exception men.

I am most familiar with Protestant seminaries—Midwestern, Eastern, Southeastern. (I understand that I could not get into a Catholic seminary.) I recently attended a consultation at a major Eastern seminary, the over-all effect of which caught up some accumulated sensory impressions of "seminaries I have known." The images had been working on me for the first day of my visit in the form of a dull headache and came to consciousness in a flash as I scanned the subtitle of a book placed in the guest rooms: "How a Puritan Institution Shaped Generations of American Men." I shall never forget how oppressed I felt by the huge leather chairs, the

so-heavy-as-to-be-immovable mahogany furniture, the dark panel-
ing studded with portraits of patriarchs of the church (their eyes
daring one to rock the boat), the all-pervasive scent of pipe tobacco
and old leather, the weight of the whole tradition solidly bound into
thousands of books.

About those books: They are, according to our cultural stereotypes, a thinking *man*'s cup of tea. I have already mentioned that
a major task of seminaries is to engage in theological reflection.
While this pastime is undergoing significant alterations in some circles, the weight of its very long tradition leans heavily toward highly
rational, systematized, philosophical (largely along Greek lines)
thought. A few years ago a philosophical journal called *Review of
Metaphysics* ran an essay contest on the question, "Why Has There
Never Been a Great Woman Philosopher?" I feel sure that few if
any men in the field (professors and theological students included)
would doubt the basic assumption behind the question for a moment or that the answers to that question are as much a part of the
"nature of things female" as is motherhood. It goes without saying
that the relentless conditioning of men and women in our culture
to disassociate the female from rational and philosophical thought
deeply affects women in seminaries.

What seems to affect the female seminarian most directly though
is that she literally as well as figuratively does not *exist* in the seminary setting. Women occur only very rarely on theological faculties
and in seminary student bodies. If they do occur, they can usually
be found in their "place," i.e., Christian nurture, Christian education, child development, and so on. If any women do come to seminaries they are generally steered into a short-term course of study
designed to help them to take better care of the churches' music,
children, heathen (in the mission field), and clergymen (as their
secretaries).

The scarcity of women on this scene makes it difficult for us to
resist either identifying with men and masculine goals or accepting
some of the fantastically stereotyped projections thrown our way by
large numbers of males working through questions of sexuality, authority, identity. In the process we get cast as Mother (good and/or
evil), Temptress, Virgin, Sister, Lover, Eros, Earth, the Unconscious—you name it. Since we are not without our own identity
crises to work through, finding out who we might really be in such
a setting and with so few "sisters" is next to impossible.

The Invisible Women

I want to say something here about the women on seminary campuses who are there in body and still do not seem to exist as far as the seminary is concerned. I'm speaking of the wives of all the men. Some seem not to have known much about what they were getting into when they married ministers-to-be, but many who leaned toward full-time vocation in the church themselves, walked easily through the only door that was wide open, and married a clergyman. The myth still abounds among seminary men that a single woman can really have no other reason for being here than to snag one of her male classmates in a setting where the odds are phenomenally in her favor.

It may seem somewhat extreme at first to say that the wife of the student (and sometimes of the faculty member) does not exist in seminaries, but the facts are that she usually works his way through school (most financial aid schedules are based on full-time employment of a married student's wife), takes care of his home, bears the beginning of his family and thanks God for her survival at the end of the three or four years. On top of all this she considers it a privilege to have been allowed to "serve" in such a way. In the meantime *he* gets a graduate education and a gap in intellectual development and experience comes between them which lasts forever. Of course this particular part of the process does enable them both to take their proper places more easily in the local church: his at the head and hers in service, with the women and children. Be all this as it may, I sense a very encouraging (at least from my point of view) rumbling among seminary wives. On our campus, for instance, this year the seminary wives association (euphemistically and degradingly called Drew Dames) went through major death throes as the women realized that "bazaars, a good meal, and an interesting program just doesn't make it." I do not think that they are wondering *only* how to be better ministers' wives any longer; they show promising signs of calling the whole role into question.

The Response of the Seminaries

Some seminaries are showing signs of a growing consciousness of the questions being raised around the relationship of male and

female to church and society. I am presently excited by it all but
have no illusions about what such beginnings can effect in the way
of basic change in a tradition and an institution hopelessly (from
most feminists' point of view) riddled with male chauvinism. My
own guess is that women's liberation will either hit the church and
seminary very hard and affect it very fast or give those institutions
up as not worth the time and energy. There are women's caucuses
springing up in many seminaries, even though there may be only
five to ten women to caucus. Once committed to defining themselves as such, they quickly start to confront administrative, faculty, and student structures with the need to do some self-examining
and changing around the woman question. They have met with
every type of response, from mutual concern to ridicule. In the
main they have run into a few nervous laughs and a brick wall of
patronizing tolerance. Of course any of these responses is accom-
panied by indignant denial of discrimination against women ("After
all some of our best friends are women") in recruitment procedures, financial aid, job placement, and so on, but until we see
some real activity in these areas for women—activity which results
in their showing up on our campuses and in our parishes in much
larger numbers—signs of officially neutral intentions are small comfort.

In trying to examine the role of women in church and society
many different approaches have been taken on seminary campuses.
Curriculum committees are not known for their lightning response
to shifting tides of social change, so most activities have been extra-
curricular in nature (i.e., films, discussions, workshops, consulta-
tions, lectures, and so on). This is certainly not good enough. We
must move soon to institute long-standing commitment to dealing
with the woman question in seminaries. It is not going to go away.
The calling into question of rigid role distinctions for both men and
women is here to stay.

If nothing else has come clear to me in seminary, it is plain that
the roots of oppression of women and men by rigid stereotyped sexual role distinctions are buried deep in the very foundations of our
religion and culture. They are not easily reached or dredged up,
but unless we attempt to get at them way down at that level we
will never find release to be whole human beings. We have dug up
a few roots around Drew and in the process have felt great hope
and great desperation. I shall tell something of the story of the

courses on the "woman thing" because I think it contains many of the elements of what promises to be a visceral crisis-struggle in the seminary-church and in the life of the culture to which Christianity is inextricably bound.

A Class Experience

A year and a half ago the only woman and in many ways the only remotely radical professor on our faculty offered a course under the title of "Equipping the Laity for Ministry; with Special Emphasis on Women" which eventually became known as the "Woman Thing." It caused quite a stir both inside and outside the classroom and was offered for a second semester under the title of "Woman in Church and Society" with the following course description:

An exploration into the rising and persistent question regarding the place of women in church and society. Once the hierarchal structures of ecclesiastical life are called into question, the freedom of men and women to come into a new humanity is opened up. An attempt will be made to examine biblical images that perpetuate the stereotypes at the same time the basic biblical confession transcends them.

She began the course by reminding us of Rosemary Ruether's description of the experience one has when one confronts and calls into question the very nature of sexual identity and sexual roles as he or she has previously understood them: "It's like picking up the ground on which we stand and shaking it." And it was!

The format was to be: reading in the general area of woman in church and society, formulating of directions for activity and/or deeper study in special areas of the question, struggling through the implications as individuals or small groups shared the results of their activity, and serious raising of issues of male and female in close and honest interaction in the classroom. (I received a real baptism of fire into this last segment of the class activities when in the first session a minister in the class expressed shock and dismay upon learning that I was a minister's wife and kept referring to my husband as "the poor fellow.")

The courses were elected by both men and women. Of course there were fewer women than men, but there were more women than one usually finds in a seminary classroom. In the second semester the course was elected by two "seminary wives"; and both courses were elected by women who were not in degree programs at Drew but were working in churches either as lay women or as professional church workers.

We all came to the course with few expectations which reflected "new feminist" influence as such. We were interested in exploring everything from group dynamics to the "handling" of women in the local church. Many were interested in exploring the general area of sexual role and identity and some even felt that sexual roles in our culture were too rigid.

We tried all kinds of approaches to the subject. There were lectures and papers delivered on such subjects as "The Biblical Narrative and Women," "Creation Stories and Women," "Myths, Memory, and Women," "I am Curious Yellow and the Woman Question," and "The Differences between Men and Women."

The classes joined chapters of the National Organization of Women for meetings in New York City and Princeton, N. J. Various ones of us consulted with all stripes of "liberationists." Two members of one of the classes made a film entitled "Women and Evil."

Some of our best insights into the role and position of professional women in the institutional church came at a consultation which three of the class members set up at the National Council of Churches offices in New York. The class met there with about fifteen women who were in some of the highest positions held by women in the institutional church. The meeting was chaired by the woman who is now president of the National Council and the opening remarks were patronizingly made by the man who is General Secretary of the Council. He opened his remarks by assuring us all that "we love our women here" and that "we could never get along without them." He had to leave the meeting abruptly when he was reminded of James Foreman and company's imminent arrival in his office. From that point there followed conversations marked by passion and unusual candor. These extremely respected and competent professional women shared with us some of their deepest anguish about the role of women, including themselves, in the church. They were living proof of the fact that a successful woman is one who has been able to do a more outstanding job in most cases than most men or she would never have been considered for a job—and they knew it:

If you get a crummy man in a job, nobody pays any attention to that. He's ordained, he's a Reverend, you know. It's okay. You put a woman in a job, and . . . if she isn't top notch, forget it . . . she can't even be average, unless of course she works for the women's organizations. It's all right to be average in there—it's what's expected of women. The minute a woman is not terribly good then she's a woman.

We did a lot of talking and "consciousness raising" throughout the course around the issue of woman in the mass media and concluded quite early that this was surely one relentless source of her most stereotyped conditioning. Two of us were interested in exploring in depth the development of an advertising campaign which made particularly blatant use of women in both image and message. We chose Virginia Slims and Silva Thins cigarettes. The Silva Thins people were about as cordial as the sadistic main character in their ads and told us in no uncertain terms that they had no interest in discussing any of their "top secret" marketing procedures. (Silva Thins' latest commentary on women continues in their fine tradition of degradation: The best cigarettes are like the best women—thin and rich.)

The Virginia Slims people, on the other hand, went out of their way to wine, dine, and woo us. They felt certain that they were contributing to woman's growing "sense" of freedom. We spent a very instructive evening with an advertising man who was very much involved in the designing and continuing development of the Virginia Slims' campaign. In a nutshell his philosophy was: advertising's business is to sense, exploit, and move forward with cultural trends; women seem to want to *feel* free now and we can sell them a cigarette if we can convince them that they will feel freer for it. He was surprised that we were not impressed that he had helped to elevate and broaden the image of women with his ads. She still looked like a high-fashion sexual object to us. Since then Virginia Slims has committed itself to the "Movement" and puts its cigarette up right alongside of Susan B. Anthony in the effort to free women. She still looks like a high-fashion sexual ornament-object to us.

Some of our most enlightened learnings came during role-playing sessions. In one, for instance, the directions were to "play" the opposite sex. One woman, who could usually be described as active, assertive, confident, competent, easily able to take the initiative, assumed the male role. The female role was taken by a quiet man, unassuming by his own admission, somewhat "passive" by our cultural standards. They were to "play out" an evening date. It was clear sailing through opening and closing of doors, ordering dinner, paying for it and other such "social customs." Things got a little rocky when the woman realized that she should ask him up to the apartment after dinner. She managed that, and offered him a drink, but she was starting to get nervous. From about that point on there was a rapid deterioration in her ability to cope. She ended up suggesting quite adamantly that she drive him home while he protested that it was much too early.

Not long after this exchange the whole "play" broke down. Both participants had been deeply affected by the feelings that had emerged. She was shocked at her inability to take initiative in the situation. She kept telling herself that it was only play-acting and she knew that what was called for was at least some mild form of sexual advance but she could not bring herself to do it. She said that she actually felt scared. He, on the other hand, found himself feeling increasingly comfortable in his role. In the first place, he said, considerable pressure was removed when he was not expected to take all the initiative. But then, as she began to break down, he felt completely in control of the situation and quite aggressive. He had no trouble putting pressure on her to continue the evening with the hope that they could pull off something romantic. He said that in "real life" he generally felt a great deal of conflict in such a situation. I had the distinct impression that one of the sources of his usual conflict was the weight of the super-masculine image laid on him by the culture and consequently by himself.

Another staged situation was especially good I think because it dealt with a subject which must receive more critical concern in the church. A first-year seminarian and his wife played the pastor and his wife in the local church. They were to calmly discuss together how they would function as a team in this particular small church situation. He was aware of her needs to set her own agenda and to be her own person; he was also not about to fall into the trap of expecting her to play the stereotyped role of servant or of the behind-every-great-man minister's wife. They pulled it off for a few minutes, but tension gradually developed as he became increasingly interested in talking about "little ways" in which she could help him while not really compromising her integrity and as she became increasingly resistant to his suggestions. He finally became quite

frustrated because, he said, she would be of no use "as a tool" to
him. The words were not out of his mouth before both the couple
and the rest of the class realized the implications of the direction
their conversation had taken.

An Impossible Role?

The fact is that there is a strong set of expectations surrounding
the minister's wife in the local church and they are as effectively institutionalized as they would be if canonized. She is to play the
woman behind the man. It is *his* ministry even if the couple per-
sists in seeing it as *their* ministry. Among other things, the woman
is expected to be her husband's liaison with the women of the
church and she may be asked to pitch in on any activity when an
extra hand is needed. (Any local church is well aware that it is
hiring two-for-the-price-of-one when it hires a married man). On
top of all this, theirs is to be the model of Christian family life for
the community and she is to see to that by raising their children
with infinitely more patience and success than other women. In all
areas she is to be an exemplary Christian woman, an image which
consists first and foremost of such qualities as servitude, meekness,
selflessness and a general curbing of any ego-centered direction in
favor of a higher authority. These are qualities which may be worth
male consideration, but they hardly warrant any more reinforcing
in the female personality structure. I seriously question the extent
to which any woman can meet these expectations without paying a
very high price in the freedom to find and express her own identity.
Of course most women who marry ministers have been well-condi-
tioned to willingly pay the price and feel no apparent loss in the
process. The fact that so few feel it makes it no less a loss that
nearly half of the people who actually staff the church never develop the ability to lead it as only a whole human being could.

Breaking Down the Stereotypes

From my point of view, the most valuable experience was con-
fronting each other as males and females and thrashing it out. I
think the women scared *themselves* as they rapidly became more
"radicalized" than they had ever counted on before the course. We
all found rage within ourselves that we thought we had long since

dealt with. Such exhortations as "just so you keep your femininity," and "the male ego is a delicate thing" were things we had heard all our lives, had lived with, and had even believed in. But after a few weeks in class we became angry when such slogans were invoked and we said so. I think the men scared themselves as their male chauvinism surfaced in defense. We all had a great deal invested in thinking that we were quite far along the road to being liberated human beings. Many of us were resisting cultural stereotypes of all kinds which we considered dehumanizing. We were at least moderate and mostly liberal on all major social issues. Most of us thought ourselves ready to get on with such things as strategy for social change and personal transformation (for others). We were shocked when confronted with the set of social stereotypes we had bought and started selling about the issue of sexual identity. One man wrote the following in his evaluation of his experience in the course:

It was a strange experience for me to learn that I looked at black persons differently than I did at whites—for years my parents had told me that it wasn't right to hate anyone for their skin color, so I believed that I wasn't prejudiced. It has been frightening to learn that I also look at women differently than men, and that until recently no one was even aware of that prejudice. Specifically, I have not been pleased to realize that my relationships with my girl friend, fellow students, and women in general are bound so much by the cultural conceptions implanted in me . . . it's a heavy thing.

Things got very personal—down to the "nitty gritty," I guess you would say. There were countless experiences not unlike the following two. In one of the early class sessions I was in a small group with one other woman and three men. I had just gotten to know one of the men in another context and we liked each other very much. We were all talking about generalized feelings we tended to have about the opposite sex. He blurted out that if he were to be really honest he would have to say that women can be thrown into one of two categories: "big and strong and little and strong; and [raucous laughter] it is unwise to turn your back on either kind." At this utterance, I think I blanched and I know my mouth fell open and he said "I guess that makes you feel funny." I not only felt funny but I think I even felt hurt. It wasn't until the next class that either of us was able to really talk about it. The other vivid memory is of the day that the men reported back to the women the results of their conference on the subject of the way the women came across in class. One of the men took this opportunity to tell us all that we were abnormal women in the first place ("Any woman in seminary just isn't like other women") and that this probably accounted for some of our strange ideas. These comments evoked general rage among the women.

These kinds of things happened "intra-sexually" as well. Of course I was not privy to a lot of the interplay among the men. There was some sparring among them though, and it usually occurred when they started to get into anything very personal like sex or their own marriages. At these junctures there would usually be a lot of joking and laughing. I always sensed an undertone of discomfort, competition and fear of having their "masculinity" questioned by another. The women could be very hard on each other at times also. In one session a younger woman who was pregnant was sharing some deeply felt ambivalences about becoming a mother. Many people in the class were becoming uncomfortable. One man felt moved to say that his wife had never felt such things and she was a wonderful mother; another man went so far as to say that a woman could never be really fulfilled unless she had a child; but the most impassioned defense made against the young mother-to-be's doubts was made by a middle-aged mother of four who feared the loss of good mothers, marriage and the family in the face of such talk. I hasten to add that at no point did the young woman say that she felt anything stronger than ambivalence about these matters, but by the time it was all over she felt just as attacked as she would have been had she given a speech in favor of the abolition of sex, marriage, and the family.

I can say with little doubt that we who have taken the course, and possibly the whole seminary, will never be quite the same. With the exception of one man whose defense against the experience was to find it laughable, everyone was willing to acknowledge some change in outlook. Nearly everyone would probably go along with most of what this person said in his evaluation: "This course has firmly exposed and damaged many cultural myths about men and women to which I had given unconscious tacit assent. It has opened my mind. I doubt that my perception can ever be the same."

The Real Question

As for the seminary as a whole, I cannot really say that I'm very optimistic. Seminary women everywhere are coming to consciousness around the general issues raised by the women's liberation movement, but there are few places where it is clearer that it is a man's world than in a seminary, and I see very few signs that men in these institutions are at all ready to take the issue seriously. On the whole the church has done precious little to distinguish itself as an institution sensitive to the deepest forms of oppression inherent in its own culture and it has done and continues to do no better on this issue of women. About the most we can discern at this point in the majority of men in the seminary community (students, faculty, and administration) is a somewhat nervous laugh accompanying a biased remark about women. On my more hopeful days I think that is a good omen but as one of my favorite budding liberationist friends would say, "That and a dime will buy you a cup of coffee."

In the final analysis the question of the seminary's ability to deal with women and the "woman question" is rendered somewhat irrelevant by the simple fact that no amount of enabling her to become a whole human being and no amount of equipping her for ministry is going to matter as long as the institution within which she is to work—the church—makes no significant place for her in its theology, function and structure. In the meantime we may discover that the energy spent in looking around for access to a place in a sinking ship would have been better spent in building a new one.

WOMEN IN THE MINISTRY

by Norma Ramsey Jones

One day during my last year at the theological seminary a woman classmate went to the school's part-time employment office to sign up for "pulpit supply." On the surface, this was a matter-of-course thing to do. One of the best ways in which a senior seminary student can gain experience in pastoral skills is weekend "supply" preaching in pastorless churches within driving distance of the campus. It goes without saying that the work provides not only experience but also a small income, something which a student in the last year of training usually needs. The woman student who requested this supply work was well qualified. She had a high academic average, having received top marks in Homiletics (sermon construction) and Preaching (sermon delivery). She was an officer of the Student Council; and, if it says anything about her ability, her family has produced some of the great preachers and leaders of my denomination.

This young woman was not sent out as a supply preacher. After several awkward moments, the official in charge of placing students in empty pulpits told her: "Really now, Miss ————, you surely can see the position you would put the seminary in. Why, we could as easily send out a Negro to preach as a woman!"

That happened in 1958, and the situation at this particular seminary has long since been remedied. Qualified women—and Negroes—are sent out under the official seminary aegis to supply pulpits. But one fears that the attitude which kept my classmate from getting to be a supply preacher is very much alive, not so much on the seminary campus as in the thought and practice of the church. It has always seemed to me that black colleagues must endure many of the same inequities and frustrations that I must—although most of them bear it with better grace! So, when I reflect upon my experiences during ten years as a woman in pastoral ministry, I do it from the point of view that some of the basic problems of blacks in church and culture are also those of women. Both are seeking greater fulfillment through redefining their traditional role.

My present situation as a graduate student probably enables me to have a fair amount of objectivity as I look back on my years in the pastorate. Since I am preparing for some form of ministry on campus, with students and faculty, it seems unlikely that I shall ever again serve as full-time pastor of a local congregation—except as "pulpit supply," which I am doing now. I have no ax to grind in my own behalf. Nor can I honestly say that I left the pastorate for doctoral study because I think it is impossible for a woman to function happily or successfully as pastor. In many ways I feel I did just that. It simply seems that *this* particular woman minister can function better on campus because of her own personal abilities, including a strong scholarly bent.

One problem in writing about these matters is that one tends to come out sounding entirely too negative, not to say positively testy! In the main, the pastorate was for me a happy and meaningful experience. And yet most of the joys I knew do not seem to have been markedly different from those experienced by my male colleagues—the satisfaction of serving, deep wonder at seeing lives changed, the endless relearning of how dependent we are upon the Lord we serve and how all-sufficient He is. And, I must add, the joys far outweigh the frustrations.

On the other hand, in order to assess my problems in the pastorate, I must divide them into two classes. While it is true that my male colleagues shared many of my woes, it is also true that I had a particular set of problems to overcome just because I am a woman. These are the problems which I think I have in common with black brothers and sisters in our society, whether or not they are ministers. Most of these problems center around the issue of one's proper role, or what is usually called "keeping in your place."

The Woman's "Place"

All the time that I served in churches I had conflicts over the exact nature of my "place." The first way in which I encountered the problem was my inability to fit into the kind of well-defined role which the church has traditionally assigned to my sex. I found myself struggling resentfully against a great many outdated behavior patterns I resented the fact that the church (of all places!) often seemed chary of permitting me the freedom to express my Christian commitment in a manner most consistent with my own abilities. For example, I resented the fact that when I would go to a new Presbytery it was immediately assumed that here they had a recruit for the Children's Work Committee. And I *resented* the *resentment* I experienced when I would say that under no circumstances was I suited to serving on Children's Work. It would be implied that a woman who would thus reject little children must necessarily be a bad woman, or at least an unnatural one. In vain did I protest that I actually *like* little children—that, in fact, some of my best *friends* are children, but that my objection to being on the Children's Work Committee arose from my ignorance of how to teach little folk. It seemed obvious to me that most of my male colleagues would have been better at this than I. They, at least, were parents!

The role conflict that I am speaking of goes much deeper than such petty matters as committee assignments. And here my resentment has sometimes been leveled, perhaps unfairly, at some of the women who have preceded me in professional church work. I have become positively ill when hearing women members of my Synod staff, far more competent and far less well paid than their male compeers, say rather self-righteously, "Of course I wouldn't *want* to be ordained!" Some capable, well-trained women church professionals may indeed feel this way. But when they say it as if they were citing some kind of personal virtue, their attitudes become suspect. Perhaps they have said it so long they really believe it. These women seemed to be saying that to be a useful female servant of the church one must deny to oneself a whole series of possibilities for service (which ordination would have opened up). A paradoxical situation!

The work of women pastors today is often hampered by woman's traditional second-class citizenship in the institutional church. Although the church has long since gotten over debating about whether or not women have souls, there still appears to be considerable confusion as to whether or not they possess minds—or skills other than the relatively menial. At least this seems to be the case when we look at the kinds of jobs which in the past have been regarded as women's work in the church. Naturally, there is nothing at all wrong with this work—cooking suppers, washing pews, teaching the children (generally considered to be more demanding physically than mentally), relief work, and even the petty shopkeeping which raises money for a variety of worthy projects. What is objectionable is that in the view of many Christians, even now, this is really *all* that women should be doing, except for the one or two "showcase" women who are graciously permitted to sit on the official boards—but who are not expected to become vigorous advocates of anything. I shall never forget the horror expressed by one of my male colleagues when I suggested that men ought to share with women in some of these necessary but unexciting tasks so that women would, in turn, be freed to make their contribution at the policy-making level. He was quite amazed that I could dare suggest that a man stoop to such tasks. And yet I'm quite sure that this same man firmly believes in the idea that the church is necessarily a co-operative fellowship of those who know that they stand equally before their Maker!

Implicit in all of these things are two mutually exclusive ideas: The first is that the *real work* of the church must be done by men, with women taking care of the lesser tasks. The second assumption is that if women were permitted to move into the power structures of the church they would "take over" and completely feminize the institution. This latter assumption is particularly fostered by male clergy whose doubts about their own masculinity are exacerbated by the many supposedly "feminine" roles into which their calling forces them, such as visiting elderly ladies in the afternoon, consoling the grieving, and working at constructing sermons and lessons rather than political or commercial enterprises. In any event, it hardly seems likely that reducing women's ability to fulfill their commitment will solve the problems of a feminized ministerial role or an emasculated church! Yet, time and again, women are told that it is their moral duty to restrain themselves from making a full contribution to the life of the church because they will thereby avoid scaring off potentially committed men.

This kind of role confusion in the total church lays the groundwork for many of the problems which women pastors experience, and which I experienced in the course of two pastorates, one a town and country parish of which I was pastor, the other a university community congregation where I was associate. Thus, the woman pastor is in for the same sort of response which was once generally accorded an "uppity nigger" who, on the basis of education and skills, dared refuse to "stay in his place." Whenever she tries to break out of the mold, she is fighting the attitudes and practices of centuries.

Role Identity

Another problem which ordained women in the established Protestant denominations must fight is the lack of role models. In fact, most of us who are in our thirties and forties *are* the role models for others to follow. Ordained in 1960, I was the seventeenth woman in the United Presbyterian Church (UPUSA) to be admitted to the ministry. Even today, when the number of ordained women in my denomination has more than trebled, only a very small number of us are actually pastors of churches. When I set out for the theological seminary I had never laid eyes on a woman minister. I met a few pentecostal "sisters" while serving my rural parish. But the first seminary trained ordained woman I ever encountered was the Reverend Dr. Mossie A. Wyker, very much a lady, and very, very sharp. Mrs. Wyker was already retired when I became acquainted with her, but she was very busy doing a study on the status of ordained women for the National Council of Churches. After two years of making my own traditions, meeting this great church stateswoman was a rare privilege.

It is possible for an ordained woman to function for years at a time without meeting others of her kind. Women Doctors of Christian Education (D.C.E.'s) are more numerous, but their attitudes are often surprisingly ambivalent toward ordained women. A part of this is no doubt caused by envy of those who have earned the "right" to be considered equal to men. Another, and more legitimate, aspect of this ambivalence is the only too well justified scorn which many D.C.E.'s have for the clergy in general due to the latter's ignorance about Christian Education. However, I must add that when properly approached, D.C.E.'s can be a gold mine of helpful information for groping young pastors. Most of what I know about Christian Education I learned from women D.C.E.'s.

Another, and again unexpected, source of role definition for ordained Protestant women is the Roman Catholic nun. Whatever have been the restrictions of their cloistered existence—and in these post-Vatican II days, many restrictions are no more—these dedicated women have the advantage of long experience in institutional self-government, and even have successfully defied powerful elements of the all-male church hierarchy. The smartest and most capable nuns I have known often evinced a kind of gentle contempt for the men who run the church. A really charming characteristic of almost all nuns is their unbeatable confidence that women do not need to depend upon men for anything in the performance of a Christian duty. I call it charming because most nuns are so pleasingly feminine as they go their unaggressive but independent way. It has often occurred to me that when the day does come when Roman Catholic women are permitted to take holy orders and function as priests they will have an enviable pattern of self-reliant feminine Christian discipleship to use for a model.

Relationships with Other Clergy

As the Protestant woman pastor develops her own sense of role identity, mostly without benefit of models, she will encounter another and even greater problem as she tries to figure out what is her "place." By nature of her training and the job she is hired to do, she must break away from the old stereotype of a "good churchwoman." But whether or not she will be able to perform successfully in her work in this new "place" is not dependent upon her alone. It will largely depend upon the way in which she is supported in her work by clerical colleagues and by laymen. In general I would assert that she can count upon more support from laity than clergy.

Before I start getting letters from my dear brethren canceling our friendship, I had better qualify. Many of my closest friends and supporters are clergymen, and since most of the clergy are male, most of these friends are male. Some of my brethren, when they first meet me, "take me up" as some liberal whites do Negroes, because they feel sorry for me. Who of us can survive without "a little help from our friends?" I'm grateful even for this kind of concern; and, in time, I usually manage to convince them that I can be a helpful friend in return. Of course, some male colleagues just take me as I am, a fellow pastor, and let it go at that; they do this, bless them, because this is the honest, open way in which they respond to every one of their fellow men. All of us should be so grown up!

On the other hand, there are a number of factors which militate against acceptance of women pastors by their male colleagues. The first is the distrust which far too many clergy have for one another. I have been at meetings of ministerial alliances in which we sniffed out one another's strengths and weaknesses with all the wary acuity of a pack of starving huskies before a fight. The loneliness of ministers and the lack of fellowship among them is one of the real tragedies of the clergy today, but this goes far beyond the scope of the problem I am dealing with here.

The fact that some men simply cannot stand the threat of female competition is also in the picture. This is the main reason why a woman may be much happier serving as pastor of her own parish rather than in the staff situation. The problems of staff ministry are treated so well elsewhere that there is no need to go into them here (*cf*. William W. Sweet, *Multiple Staff in the Local Church*). It is quite possible, we must note, that an insecure senior pastor may prefer a woman colleague, feeling that she will be a lot easier to keep in what he thinks is an assistant's "place."

Although I suggest that a woman pastor is most likely to function happily in a parish of her own, today's problem is that it is becoming increasingly difficult for *all* ministers to move into parishes of their own which present more challenging opportunities. As the statisticians have been telling us for a long time, institutional American Christianity is in a state of decline or "recession." Working pastors know it by the decrease in membership and attendance and budget. Older pastors know it because many of them are not going to move up to that larger congregation which was to have climaxed a lifetime of service. Instead, they are wondering whether they can even make a lateral move—to a parish of the same size where new and different aspects of ministry will keep them from going stale. Younger pastors are finding it difficult to make even modest upward moves. This is not to say that the desire to change and move on is the fruit of sinful ambition. Very often this ambition is very Christian. It is not so much a desire for more money—although a desire for additional income on the part of a man with two or three college educations to finance is understandable, to say the least. But more than money, what is needed is a greater challenge, an opportunity to put the experience and judgment one has gained in a smaller sphere to work for the good of the larger.

What all of this does mean for women ministers is that when

pastors are having a hard time finding opportunities to move into more challenging jobs, women pastors will have the hardest time of all. Thus, the woman who might best be suited to being pastor of her own parish may well be condemned to choosing between a pastorate in a sleepy rural hamlet where nothing is happening and a staff position. In the most literal sense, the only possible way out of this dilemma is through prayer. Furthermore, in view of the relevant new forms of *koinonia* and ministry which are now evolving as the church is forced by the present "recession" to consider the failures of its institutional life, one cannot help but feel confident that new doors to ministry will be opening for women. Such new doors are probably not yet dreamed of by most of us who have not begun to catch up with the Christ who is always out there moving ahead of us. It may even be that many future ministers and theologically trained laymen, male and female, will earn their bread at secular jobs in order to be economically free to engage in that form of ministry to which they are most deeply committed. In the meantime, many women ministers will be faced with the hard choice between moribund rural parish and staff ministry which I have described.

There is one particular caution which should be exercised by every woman pastor who contemplates becoming part of a church staff. If she is not and does not want to become a specialist in Christian Education, she should make this very clear at the outset. Even so, and despite the fact that her degree is in theology, many hiring committees think that when they hire a woman minister they are really getting an ordained D.C.E. Congregations should be particularly wary of hiring an ordained woman if their greatest need is in the area of education for the reason that, if the woman were especially interested in that kind of work she would have taken her degree in Education rather than in preparation for regular pastoral ministry. The B.D. or S.T.B. degree is usually a dead giveaway that the woman thinks of herself as a pastor rather than a Christian Educator. She probably likes to preach and do counseling and run the church. Unless she makes a definite statement to the contrary, she should not be hired to do work for which a D.C.E. is better qualified. This is even more important in view of the fact that all too many congregations still think of Christian Education as "children's work." A crafty, aggressive D.C.E. is usually able to begin by doing children's work and then branch out into adult education where the real educational catastrophe in the church exists. A woman pastor who isn't devoted to Christian Education may not have the skills or the patience to do the infiltration job which is needed in such situations.

Response of the Laity

To return to the problem of acceptance, it should not be too surprising that a woman pastor is more readily accepted by laymen than by the clergy. This is particularly true, it should be added, if she is pastor of a church of her own. After all, to whom else can the poor layman turn for pastoral services? Unless he be a violent misogynist, he will seek out the help of his own pastor first, even though she is a woman. Not only is she the pastor of his church, she also has a degree in theology, plus the denominational stamp of approval by virtue of the fact that she is ordained. Once given the chance to serve—however she gets that chance—the woman pastor is usually able to gain the respect of the layman. Some of the dear souls may even become rather proud of the fact that they have something a bit unusual in their pulpit! Others will cite their acceptance of the lady shepherd as a symbol of how tolerant they are. But even more important than these reasons, the woman pastor will find the laymen ready to accept her just because she is a pastor. She will fall heir to a great treasury of affection and respect which has been built up by the dedicated ministers—mostly men—who have gone before her. Whatever they would have thought, during their lifetime, of sermonizers in skirts, it is to be hoped that they are now willing to have their daughters share in that honorable legacy.

Finally, it is my opinion that if female clergy are more easily accepted by laymen than by other clergy, it is also true that a woman pastor will likely be more acceptable to men than to women parishioners. One always makes this statement with great apprehension. What is meant, of course, is that the *small minority* of laymen who will not accept a woman as their pastor is composed largely of women. This is not, I am sure, because men are just naturally more apt to give other people a fair chance. I think the reason lies much deeper, in the personal needs of some of the women with whom the pastor will work. Some capable, independent-minded wives and mothers really resent the fact that they are "tied" to home and hearth while their pastor leads the glamorous life of a professional woman. They are too sorry for themselves to realize that swapping places with the pastor would be trading a mild headache for a migraine! If the pastor gets to know these women at all well, she can usually win them over just by telling them what a day in her "glamorous" life is *really* like. In quite a different category is the woman who resents her female pastor because in her life the minister has always filled the role of substitute father. Now, here is Mommy, in the form of the lady pastor, usurping Daddy's place once again. There isn't much the pastor can do about this kind of female parishioner except pray—and hope that she doesn't do too much talking behind the pastor's back! On the other hand, for some women, who didn't get along with Daddy, the woman pastor is the answer to a great many unfulfilled needs. There is only room in this article for this brief nod in the direction of Freud, but we must emphasize that one of the real lacks in American Protestant ministry in the past has surely been the dearth of female religious authority figures with whom troubled individuals might communicate. The increase in the number of women pastors will undoubtedly be a help to those men and women who find it easiest to have rapport with a woman in the counseling situation.

In conclusion, it should be obvious that this essay is only a beginning list of significant factors related to women in parish ministry. For the future, one can only foresee continuing conflict in this area. A male denominational executive once told a woman minister friend of mine that he was proud of the fact that he had fought so hard for women to be ordained to the ministry in my church. However, he added, his fighting days are over where this cause is concerned. He would do everything in his power to pull down "barriers" against women; but having done that for them, the women were to be on their own. The mind boggles at the sight of such naïveté on the part of one of the most distinguished churchmen of our time. Like our black brethren, we women ministers are rapidly discovering that the removal of legal barriers to the fullest expression of humanity and service is only the beginning of the fight. The years ahead will show whether we will be able to break out of the social and cultural straitjacket in which we have been bound up.

THE SISTERS JOIN
THE MOVEMENT

Statements by the Sisters of the
Immaculate Heart of Mary, Los Angeles

These two statements from the 1967 Decrees of the Chapter of Renewal, Sisters of the Immaculate Heart in Los Angeles, constitute a framework of ideals for the effort of these women to determine their life and work within the structure of the Roman Catholic Church. While they are the official position only of the order in Los Angeles, the spirit of the statements pervades many religious orders, and sisters have begun to question their future in the essentially male-dominated church. The depth of the problem is indicated by the news article which follows the two documents. It appeared in The Catholic Voice *of Oakland, California, on January 28, 1970. While this decision to work outside canonical structures is part of a picture of growing concern among both men and women in religious orders, it takes on an added dimension in the present context of women's efforts to participate in a full and meaningful way in the life of the church.*

Prologue

We live in an era marked by decreasing formalism and increasing candor; more and more things are being called by their names. We see the world, with its mixture of beauty and sadness, as *the only one we know and the only place in which we may live and work.* We see the church as the extension of Christ's body, instituted by Himself, meant to be of service and a yoke to no man. Christ came that we might have life, and He showed us by His own choices, by unhesitatingly transcending traditional categories and separations, that life is to be abundantly fulfilled only in the freedom to make difficult and consequential decisions which confound some of the people at least some of the time.

Women, perhaps especially dedicated women, insist on the latitude to serve, to work, to decide according to their own lights. Our community's history from its beginning, including its early missionary activities in California and its eventual separation from a Spanish foundation which was inevitably removed from and indifferent to peculiarly American conditions, speaks of our readiness to abandon dying forms in order to pursue living reality. It expresses, also, our willingness to seek human validity rather than some spurious supernaturalism.

Women around the world, young and old, are playing decisive roles in public life, changing their world, developing new life styles. What is significant about this new power for women is not that it will always be for the good, nor that it will always edify, but that there can be no reversing of it now. Women who want to serve and who are capable of service have already given evidence that they can no longer uncritically accept the judgment of others as to where and how that service ought to be extended. American religious women want to be in the mainstream of this new, potentially fruitful, and inevitable bid for self-determination by women.

What all of this affirms is the pulpit message often preached but seldom perceived, that we have not here a lasting city, that we are pilgrims on the move. We must be ready to weigh the value of any change, and ready to choose it without regard to the cost, if such change appears to be in order. This is not to canonize change for its own sake, but to insist that change be rational and directed rather than happenstance and reactive, for there is no life without change. The question is whether we will ourselves determine the course of change, or submit to it passively.

Epilogue

Our Vocation as persons in community implies first of all a realization of our humanity, not an escape from it. For only in community does the human person adopt a life pattern of creative response to circumstances. Even more does the religious community involve the person in a permanent engagement with the world, rather than flight from the world or protection from its concerns. For witness to the risen Christ is given in self-sacrificing service to the world. And the best service we can bring to our industrial, urban, mechanized society is the creation of community.

Though our pilgrimage may be through space or time or continuum of ideas, the essence of our pilgrim state is the inability to rest in the status quo, with the consequent insecurities and limitations this journey may bring. This theme of search inherent in the pilgrim church does not contradict the intentional creation of community, but expands it. Community no longer carries the image of fixed abode but rather signifies the working out of ever new relationships in varied contexts.

Those who search for ways to build community cannot be strangers to change. They must not only be open to change but also imaginative and resourceful in creating this new type of community in the midst of profound change. For this task, each member needs the shared experience of Christian community. This strengthens the individual with the personal courage necessary for a life painfully open to awareness of need. Support from fellow religious is given and received in communal genuineness, friendship and loyalty. Since such experience is rare to modern life, our religious community chooses to create community today by opening itself to others, by becoming a community without walls, by relating to the larger community in varied, complex and rich ways. Interaction at first will be chiefly within the newly expanded religious community where the situation will provide the place for interaction on many levels. But those who share such human, religious, intellectual and liturgical resources will then move out into other areas of life and work with incentive and direction for forming community life wherever they are.

Our religious community becomes thus a witness to Christ by being a witness to community. It assists society at the very point where the tensions are greatest. It shows the beauty of cohesiveness, the intelligence of the common effort. It can offer useful patterns for interpersonal relationships, for building common life.

Where the religious community becomes complacent, indifferent to mankind's need for communal life, for the reassurance of brotherhood, there is infidelity and abdication of the group vocation. The faithful religious community bases its hope for renewal of society on man's search for a new social reality, a search for peace, reconciliation, and communal love.

We would miss much of the world's wonder if we were to suppose that change is limited to the measurable: production rates, population growth, the phenomenal increase in the power of lethal weapons. But these measurable elements of growth are seen in a less overwhelming perspective when we compare them with the potential significance of changing modes of communicating and learning, of new dimensions in awareness of self, awareness of others, and, ultimately, awareness of God. It would seem that the ability to change, to evaluate and direct change, must soon become prized human goals if we are not to become a generation of automata, controlled by an array of forces of change—political, technological, ideological.

Most active religious communities, including our own, had their origin in the spontaneous response of sensitive men and women to particular needs in their society which were not being adequately met: teaching and healing the poor; providing for the indigent, the destitute and dying, the incurable; catechising; witnessing to the church's concern for the life of the mind in higher education and scholarship. It was the work, and the way in which the work was done, which attracted new members to these communities, and in time the work became more or less fixed.

At the same time these communities tended to become less responsive to new and more acute needs in their societies. Their zeal had bounds set on it by their commitments to tasks no longer clearly needed, and to tasks which were being performed on a more comprehensive and far-reaching basis by agencies funded by public monies. Even buildings themselves, some of them highly specific in terms of the kind of work which could be performed in them, set limits on the apostolic imagination of those who had come to religious life in order to serve their neighbors as simply and directly as possible.

It can be confidently asserted that there is a providence in the events and trends of church and world in the last ten years as these affect members of religious communities. The documents of Vatican II summarize the spirit of these events and trends in their emphasis on the centrality of Christ, on the unity of the human community, on a renewed conception of the dignity of man and of the respect which must be paid to the voice of the Spirit speaking through human history.

Again and again, these documents recall the church and its members to Christ's intention in establishing the church: "to give witness to the truth, to rescue and not to sit in judgment, to serve and not to be served."

The pilgrim quality of the church is undeniably affirmed. The injunction to travel light is implicit in this, as is the willingness to listen to the outcry of man who, generation after generation, finds himself in the position of destroying his young, denying access to the truth, neglecting the neglected, despising the ignorant, fearing the man who is different in color and belief.

In all of this, religious today hear a desperate cry for their relevant response. By relevant the world means a response which really touches its need for peace, which leads to an end to the senseless amassing and destructive use of lethal weapons, for an end to the artificial separations of the colored peoples of God's one human race, for an end to the legalistic, judgmental, self-serving exclusions of beliefs, customs and conditions not corresponding to our own.

What the world desperately needs is bridges, individuals and groups who, like Christ himself, put an end to all the distances which divide men and which hinder their access to truth, dignity and full human development. This is another way of saying that the world needs community; it needs models of community to convince it that the diverse and warring elements in the human family can be reconciled.

Implicit in the will-to-community is a readiness to respond and a desire to move on. These become a demanding discipline and asceticism, and endow with renewed meaning the life of the evangelical counsels. They reconstitute the religious life as an effective and affective expression of service and praise. They are the voice of our founder speaking clearly again in our own time through the church to the world.

The virtue and talents and inner strength of our community give hope that we will endure and continue to contribute significantly to church and world. The will and ability to serve implicit in this hope depend upon the widening or removal of some of the institutional bounds currently set on apostolic zeal.

We wish to remain faithful to our long-standing and beneficial commitments to teaching and healing. There are some, however, who can no longer see the compatibility between the spirit of Vatican Council II and parochial education when it is conducted in such a way that the generally accepted aims of education are obstructed, or with healing as it is exercised in hospitals which are often caught in bureaucratic entanglements. There are aspects of both which seem to them to have little to do with charity or religion, with the city of man or the city of God.

The documents and decrees which follow say some introductory things about some of the changes which we believe must be made if our life and work are to be satisfying and significant and worthy to be called religious. They have to do with the spirit in which we are to render service (apostolic works, education, health services, other works); with the spirit in which we live together (person in community) and pray to our Father (apostolic spirituality); with the spirit and regulations by which we live in common according to the counsels (local and general government); with the spirit and manner in which we incorporate new members (preparation for life in community); with the whole manner in which we give "splendid witness" by our communal life and service to our faith in the possibility of fulfilling the two great commandments.

IHMS TO CONTINUE
AS LAY GROUP

Because the Vatican Congregation for Religious has refused to recognize the course of renewal chartered by the Immaculate Heart Sisters, more than 350 of them have asked the Holy See to be dispensed from their canonical vows. While 37 will leave religious life altogether, some 315 intend to form what they themselves call "a lay community of religious persons living according to the spirit of our 1967 decrees." Such a move by so many is unprecedented in church history. In a quiet, cordial meeting last week Archbishop Timothy J. Manning of Los Angeles met with Sister Anita Caspary, head of the IHM Sisters, and announced that he had been commissioned by the Holy See to grant all the requested dispensations. (In the Catholic Church religious women take public vows of poverty, obedience and celibacy. Canonical means that they conform to certain prescriptions of church law.)

According to informed sources close to the Immaculate Heart Sisters, the new IHM community will take some sort of private vows or promises and will continue their apostolic works of teaching, hospital and social work. They will continue to make their headquarters in Los Angeles. The five Immaculate Heart Sisters who teach in Corpus Christi elementary school in Piedmont will join the new lay community and continue to staff the school. A more precise announcement as to the form the new IHM community will take is expected to be made next week. It was the 1967 decrees which brought the Immaculate Heart Sisters into public controversy with conservative Cardinal James Francis McIntyre who announced his retirement last week. (Cardinal McIntyre had objected to the decisions on dress, life style and apostolate which the majority of the IHM Sisters had overwhelmingly voted to adopt following the spirit of renewal engendered by the Second Vatican Council.)

After a long dispute which received world-wide publicity, the Congregation for Religious backed Cardinal McIntyre and refused even to acknowledge or answer official correspondence from the IHM Sisters. During the controversy the IHMs split into two groups. Some 480 voted to stay with the progressive experiment (more than 100 have left since), while 50 voted to return to the traditional style of life. The minority group is expected to be sanctioned by the Vatican as an official religious community.

Sources close to the Immaculate Heart Sisters say that the move to a lay community will be described as a "creative opportunity for desperately needed new forms of religious life." But there was a touch of irony in the last letter to Cardinal Ildebrando Antoniutti, head of the Congregation of Religious, when the IHM Sisters said: "We had hoped that our sincerity in following the mandates of Vatican II would be apparent to you and the the Sacred Congregation. Since our efforts to expand the structure of canonical religious life have evidently not met with your approval, we intend now as a non-canonical group, to continue our lives as dedicated people in the manner which seems to us most fruitful and most faithful to our call."

The Catholic Voice, January 28, 1970

AN AUTHORITY OF POSSIBILITY FOR WOMEN IN THE CHURCH

by Peggy Ann Way

My concern is how a woman, deeply rooted in the profoundly theological issues with which women's liberation is involved, is to understand the authority of her ministry. My argument is that the authority of *my* ministry is in my rooted participation as a free and emerging person engaged in examining the processes of human existence, testing out their principles and traditions, and experiencing the possibilities of new creations of persons, institutions and cultures.

My ministerial authority, then, is what I am going to call the "authority of possibility," which is by no means a uniquely feminine understanding of ministry but should stand by itself as one frequently overlooked source of ministerial authority. Thus the fact of my historic exclusion from the traditional sources of authority and my need to look elsewhere as I seek to serve my God, may, as we look to the future together, serve as an unexpected source of insight into the nature of that authority by which we all seek to serve.

Let me begin by looking at three traditionally accepted sources of ministerial authority, in each of which I, as a woman minister, choose *not* to find my essential validation. The reasons for this "definition by negatives" should become clear as we progress. And, for the careful reader, their very real authenticity as possible future sources of authority for the woman in ministry should begin to emerge. The three sources through which I shall move toward my positive statement are: the Scriptures; church history; and denominational or ecclesiastical sanction.

Scriptures

I do not understand my authority as resting in the Scriptures. I have not found it helpful to do a complete rewriting of the Scriptures from a women's liberation perspective. This is, first of all, foreign to my own biblical perspective that the integrity of the Scriptures has a place of its own; and I am very uncomfortable whenever anybody rewrites the Scriptures to support a particular point of view. Thus I am as uncomfortable when I use the Scriptures to illustrate my own position as I am when the men in the church quote Jesus to support them in a variety of one-dimensional affirmations or negations.

But, more important, I understand that the root issues of scriptural interpretation are quite different from being able to quote St. Paul from a women's liberation perspective—that is, to point out what St. Paul *really* meant (which probably was not what was in 2 Corinthians!). I am myself quite at home with the fact that St. Paul probably was not very enthusiastic about women in key leadership roles in a church so imminently expecting fulfillment, and that certainly his culture affected his statements about us. The root issues, then, are not how I am to isolate quotes from St. Paul, but how the themes of the Bible are to be clarified, and who is to develop the hermeneutical principles out of which these biblical themes are explicated, developed, and communicated to ongoing generations of persons claiming allegiance to the Christian faith.

Now some themes of the Old and New Testaments are, very frankly, not my themes; that is, they are not the particular themes which I, as a woman concerned with ministry, can draw out and use as mine. There are themes with a biblical perspective which I can criticize; there are hidden themes that have not been in historical prominence recently which I could lift up, were I a biblical scholar; there are themes which have been out of fashion which I could help to re-mythologize. But as a woman, I am primarily interested in the principles of interpretation by which the Bible is to be viewed and to be a participant in the sorting-out processes by which culturally laden themes are identified.

Let me illustrate by turning to a particular example. Recently I read the Missouri Synod Lutheran position on the ordination of women,[1] because I thought it would be fun to go to the clearest point at which churchmen were presenting biblical reasons against the ordination of women. I wanted to be clear myself as to what these reasons are, stated in their most extreme form, thinking that I might well learn something about the residue of historic understandings which seems to affect even sophisticated churchmen when they find themselves forced to cope concretely with me and my sisters . . . and all those who would be our sisters were real doors to be opened to them.

What I discovered was reason for great respect for the men of the Missouri Lutheran Church because, from what I could tell as I read their understandings, they only embody with honesty what almost every churchman I know believes anyway. It is just that the Missouri Synod men have simply written it all down and stated it in clear conceptual categories. They explicate and they give roots to the present images and themes by which most men in the church understand women. For even though the rhetoric of the men with whom I work is quite clearly not Missouri Synod Lutheran (in fact, most churchmen I know would be insulted at the thought), their attitudes and actions indicate that there is a tremendous gap between their rhetoric and their mode of operation. Not the least factor in this gap appears related to their earlier indoctrination in scriptural utterances about women, which is supported and enhanced by a deep-seated cultural view of women that appears not to have changed much since the time of Paul.

The Missouri Synod men are very clear that women can never be ordained. The order of creation established the supraordination of men and the subordination of women, rooted in fixed sexual roles throughout the historical process. These sexual roles are not understood culturally or sociologically, but as rooted in the Law and, therefore, ontological and inevitable at any period of history. With such a view it is not surprising that, for them, any consideration of the ordination of women must threaten the very nature of historical revelation. (I must admit that this gives me a great sense of power!)

Now I respect this statement because I think that the Missouri Synod men who write it and say it are much more honest than most of the men of the church who argue from other points of view but act (and this is to me most crucial) as if they were indeed deeply rooted in Missouri Synod theology and in a Missouri Synod hermeneutic.

Let us look at the implications of such a point of view, whether held openly or concealed deep within the masculine consciousness. Theologically, my sexual nature becomes identified with my human spirit. While men are quite free to be other than sexual beings, my sexuality determines my spirit and my freedom. Their spirits can soar, they can engage in fascinating theological dialogue and claim and protect their "rightful" role as interpreters of the Faith, they can perform the offices of the church, and they can function in the decision-making processes. But my spirit is not free to soar and to engage in such activities and experiences because I am identified with my sexuality. Theologically my nature and my spirit have been meshed, in such a way that I am prevented from being a fully productive human being, free to serve God in as many diverse ways as any masculine human creature.

Certainly the Missouri Synod men do not denigrate women. Indeed, I was quite taken by the high esteem shown for us. Article after article had some such statement as: "We do not mean by this position to lessen our esteem for the role of women." It took the University of Chicago Divinity School faculty eighty-five years to find a woman they felt was of a high enough order to join their faculty. It had nothing to do with their lack of esteem for women— they just never could find one. Most churchmen, exclusive of my Missouri Synod friends, esteem women highly; they just don't want any around. And, like their Missouri Synod brethren, they recognize the vast diversity of *service* roles in which women should minister in the church. Thus do we continue to be recognized in categories which overwhelmingly reflect a view of the order of creation in which men are supraordinate and women subordinate, in which women's natures are fixed in terms of sexual roles, to the lessening of the full potentiality of the human spirit, a view which is denied only when it appears in a form so apparent as in the Missouri Synod hermeneutic.

Perhaps sensing that their ontological argument is under some pressures for revision, my Missouri Synod brethren also argue functionally. That is, if women were to be ordained, there could be no further renewal within the church because the divisiveness which would occur would be so intense that the renewal processes would be minimized. To date, those denominations that do ordain women seem to have experienced the divisiveness coming from quite other sources indeed, particularly when our numbers, opportunities for education, vocational options, and so on, have remained so controlled. But once again there is agonizing similarity in the cries of churchmen who don't know what to do with women who are ordained. The answer is too often to ordain as few as possible rather than to develop creative and significant opportunities for women. Are we, perhaps, dealing with a masculine consciousness that is more Missouri Synod Lutheran than the brothers are able to admit?

I suggest that churchmen remain so unself-consciously rooted in biblical world views about the nature of masculinity and femininity that the themes hold and control actions even when the authority base is denied or shifted to a more sophisticated hermeneutic. For in a very real sense the biblical statements are accidental to the understanding of primary sexual identification in many societies throughout history; and from my point of view, the sophistication of the hermeneutic or how you line up quotations from the Old and New Testaments doesn't matter. The Missouri Synod themes are those that pervade the church. Shall we women spend our time developing nice little papers on what Paul really meant or how he would speak in a different cultural setting, or, on another level, discovering that he was once in love with a temple prostitute who rejected him and from which came his feelings about women? I am afraid that I do this kind of thing myself. I can preach a sermon demonstrating how there are several creation stories and that what really counts is that God created persons instead of men and women. But I am not really sure that that is what Yahweh was understood to have been about, and there remains a certain beautiful integrity about the creation of woman from Adam's rib. Clearly there has been uncountable damage done to feminine existence because of the ways in which this myth has been transmitted and used, but the myth itself has a kind of cultural integrity that we have to learn how to look at and deal with rather than to simply rewrite. And does this, after all, touch the order of masculine consciousness with which we seem to be dealing?

Let me depart from my central argument for a moment to suggest that the authority of Scripture is important in a political sense for women in the church today. After a lengthy process of discovering that there were no scriptural reasons why women should not be ordained (and, as interpreted by some persons, no scriptural reasons why they *should* be) the Lutheran Church of America changed its terminology in order to provide for the ordination of women. The political use of Scripture was without question valuable in gaining this end.

And it is only politic to recognize that ongoing interpretation among the laity is, to some extent and with some constituencies, heavily weighted with the need for scriptural clarification. After all, even our sophisticated laity in the Presbyterian and United Churches have been systematically taught that women do not quite belong, and they see little evidence to indicate otherwise. This will not be cleared up by fiat; after all, most of our laity do not even know what a hermeneutic is!

My concern is much more profound: regardless of scriptural base or principle of interpretation, the prevailing cultural mode and visible actions seem to argue that the masculine consciousness holds to such views as the supraordination of men and the subordination of women, fixed sex roles, identification of nature and spirit, and a high esteem for women in their proper places. I am uncertain that argument on the scriptural level will deal with these views any more than scriptural argument has realistically affected issues having to do with race and peace. And I am just as uncertain that the authority of these same Scriptures makes much difference in the validation of my own ministry, or that these are the primary issues with which I choose to grapple at the present.

Nevertheless, I call upon my sisters who do make that choice to so immerse themselves in biblical scholarship that they are as competent in dealing with the methodological issues of the Scriptures as are our brothers and, in the process, find their own avenue of contribution to the broad task of defining the relevance of the Scriptures in today's church. I urge them further to focus upon creative education of the laity in the interpretation and use of the Scriptures. I call upon biblical departments to seek out women scholars and to support them as they do male students, validating in practice what some of their hermeneutics might suggest as possible and creative.

I myself do not consider that my authority as a minister in the church of Jesus the Christ is rooted in the Scriptures. Indeed, I am open to the possibility that both the Scriptures and the prevailing tone of cultural development, expressed even in the 1970s, denies me such authority. It is not a matter which the Scriptures and the culture can decide for me or confer upon me.

Church History

I do not consider church history to be the primary support for the authority of my ministry within the church. Indeed, were I to do so, I would find myself bereft of such support. Precisely as the masculine consciousness is deeply embedded within the cultures and disciplines of scriptural analysis, so is it controlling of the content and methodologies of the historical disciplines.

There are two particular tendencies within the usual modes of historical analysis that I would call to the attention of women in the church. The first of these is the way that the historical record defines, builds upon, perpetuates and creates myths about women which become the untested "self-evidents" of history. The second is the tendency of church history and the historical process in general to neglect the actual presence of real women so that there is a paucity of literature defining and tracing our actual roles within any particular historical epoch. Corollary to both of these is a somewhat sentimental approach that lumps us together in separate treatments, quite apart from the main thrusts of interpretation and methodology. What are these "self-evidents" of history, and where might we begin to create and re-create our own historical understandings? Let us look very briefly into both of these profound questions.

I am moving toward an understanding of ministry as focused around the discernment of the myths and world views by which persons live, with the minister being an agent of disclosure of the values, processes and life styles of human existence. People who know something about myth tell me that there are no new myths; there are, rather, primary and secondary myths which are raised to different levels of consciousness during different historical epochs. In relation to church history, I am interested in raising up for disclosure and discernment those myths about women which have become so much of our historical self-consciousness that they control us without our becoming aware of them as visible forces that affect our human freedom.

Let me suggest a few, and try to interest you in these historical "self-evidents" which we have failed to make visible and, therefore, to analyze and evaluate.

One is the myth of "woman as temptress," which runs through the Missouri Synod literature. It is rooted in the Fall, for which a woman is held responsible, and carries with it throughout history the idea of punishment for sexual transgression in the form of painful child rearing and being limited to the acting out of a clearly defined sexual role. I suggest that a whole myth structure about women as temptress pervades even our contemporary understandings, finding itself embodied in such specifics as rules about pastors being alone with women. The woman is not to be trusted; she will seduce the pastor. The woman is not to be on seminary faculties; the men do not know what to do with her.

What we have not dealt with is what this myth tells us about men. Why do they not know what to do with us apart from sexual fantasizing—or action? Or what does the Adamic myth tell us about the strength of men who are so easily seducible, and possibly so out of touch with their own sexuality that a gigantic myth structure must seek to keep us in our places, and so not present to tempt them? Why is our historical role so frequently limited to the woman in bed with the Great Man or, in a variety of Old Testament adaptations, busy seducing him from his rightful role as King?

If such myths suggest masculine fears of their own identity, it is not surprising that the myth of the "woman on a pedestal" has been of such historical prominence. There she cannot be touched as a full human being. She is safe, detached, perfect—and as deprived of her freedom as is the temptress. Men are free to admire and to worship—but not to touch; to idealize and romanticize—but not to participate in mutually satisfying human relationships.

The myth of the "eternally feminine woman" is complementary to this. Eternally feminine virtues like tenderness and self-denial, joy in satisfying others and steadfastness are deeply rooted within us; and, in the present context, men so fear shattering these images that they are not open to discussing other understandings of what it means to be feminine. Again, I suggest that we could learn as much about men from a serious pondering of these myths as they tell us about how cultures have imaged women.

Nor is it accidental that a series of "behind-every-great-man" or "sharing sufferer" myths pervades historical consciousness about women. Mrs. Nixon supports the decisions that her husband makes. It is her role to build him up, not to intrude upon his masculine areas, and to embody publicly a role of service and care for children, for those affected by natural disasters, and for the privacy of the family. The "receptive vehicle" myth, deeply rooted in the concept of the Virgin, is not foreign to this. The woman receives, unquestioning and without her full participation. The effects of such a myth upon generations of women experiencing their sexuality as recipients rather than active participants are only recently being called into question. The research on sexual behavior done by Masters and Johnson shows very clearly that women in the sexual act are not passive, receptive vehicles. Nor are the women in women's liberation, nor my own seminary students—whose attempts to develop their own self are so surprising to men who have never questioned the historical myths about women by which we live.

There are evidences of a "virgin queen" myth, bringing together the virginal image with that of the queen who rules. This one is upheld by men who say that women really rule the country anyway and they can't understand what all the fuss is about. The "tender tyrant" myth rules many homes, along with the "menopausal mystery" myth which speaks loudly about cultural fears of blood and argues strongly against women's emotional capacity to engage in decision-making. Again, whose emotions do these myths suggest that we should really fear?

A vast reservoir of myths about women runs through cultural and church history, their power unrecognized and their reality untested. Yet do we not still hold to a symbolic point of view that women are unclean for twice as long when they bear a girl child, and that David had better not get too close to a woman or it will affect his capacity to rule? How are such myths to be isolated, discerned, made visible, called to attention, even raised to the prominence necessary for introducing other dimensions into the historical hermeneutic?

The second tendency within church history requires us to begin to deal with our real exclusion from the historical record, in ways similar to those that minority groups have pursued in repossessing the facts of their histories and, consequently, new sources for identity. Who were the real women of history, and what contributions were they making at different periods of history which have not been accurately or adequately conceptualized? One of my students, Barbara Lane, has looked at the treatment accorded women in the writings of Kenneth Scott Lautourette. She finds that, in his early book, *The Christian World Mission in Our Day,* "he does not mention the women's missionary boards or societies specifically nor

does he consider any of the women missionaries. His later volumi-
nous work entitled *Christianity in a Revolutionary Age* contains
some references to women, but the treatment is superficial." [2] Surely
this is suggestive of the importance of looking at church history to
sort out not only the myths that are present, but also the vacuums
that speak eloquently of what has been excluded.

Another example we might take from the black community.
Black scholars are "discovering" that Harriet Tubman, for example, wasn't just a pleasant, warm, loving Negro mammy, caught up
in service and care, but was a strong revolutionary leader in her
particular cultural period. How many women are there who either
don't appear in the historical record or appear there in ways already mythologized by the masculine consciousness?

Thus I am not here interested in dealing with what Tertullian
really believed as distinct from what he said, or sorting through the
imperfect biological knowledge of Thomas Aquinas, or dealing
with the castration fears of St. Augustine, or determining why it
was that some theologians in the past, notably Luther, have taken
the position that it is quite all right for women to preach if there
are no men around—but certainly the Holy Spirit will make sure
that there are plenty of men around. I am not interested in church
history as a source of authority for my ministry, but as a vehicle
of disclosure, by which myths are lifted up to visibility and real
persons appear in the historical record. The futures of women in
church history are promising, indeed.

As a notation to these comments about history, let me add that
men are also held captive to certain myths about masculinity, not
the least of which is the felt right to phrase all theological writing
in the masculine gender. On a different level, the writings of Val-
orie Goldstein are suggestive. Perhaps one of the reasons that pride
has been such a high concept in the orthodox tradition is that it
tends to be an aspect of masculine experience, related to men's
activities and aggressiveness in the world. Thus there has been a
strong identity between pride and sinfulness. For women, however,
sinfulness might be more appropriately related to lack of pride and
self-affirmation, and unquestioning acceptance of roles where responsibilities for church and world are severely limited. The history of Christian thought is rich in potentiality for discovering such
insights, which would themselves stand as significant contributions
to the ongoing theological enterprise.

So I do not claim church history as a primary source of my ministerial authority. I do claim the right for women to be significant historians and affirm the contributions that could be made to the history of thought itself were we to depart from a strictly masculine hermeneutic.

Church Structure

As another possible source for my ministry, I might look to the bureaucracies, the denominational decision-makers, the Establishment, as my students would say. Ivan Illich is widely understood as distinguishing between "the church *she*" (to which he is committed even when he leaves it) and "the church *it*." I want to suggest that "the church it" is not in any way a source of my authority for ministry.

It may be important at this point for me to trace briefly my relationships with the church-related bureaucracies and decision-making processes, because I am not a stranger to them. I have been co-pastor of a local church, have taught at two seminaries, have been in administrative positions with the Chicago City Missionary Society (Community Renewal Society)–Northeast Association of the United Church of Christ, have been on the faculty of the Urban Training Center, and am presently serving as national chairman of the Council for Church and Ministry of the United Church of Christ. I have been richly gifted with the opportunity for bureaucratic participation, and have been similarly blessed with being present during the church history of the past ten years.

And yet I do not look with hopefulness to these structures nor do I choose to allow them to sanction my ministry. I find that as one partakes of what is meant by being a "liberated woman," one becomes freer to share what it has meant to be a woman within the church. My parish experience was within a small, dying church, which reflects the general experiences of those women who choose the parish. Even now, I would doubt that significant parishes would be open to me as head pastor. I have experienced myself as everybody's low priority. Several of my jobs have emerged because someone was needed to "fill in," and all of them have required me to work through my role as woman within a masculine setting, thus utilizing creative energies that might well have been placed in the service of broader ministry. Thus I understand myself as an accident in the church rather than a symbol of openness to women or a validation of women's great future in a variety of forms of ministry. Because I am of an earlier generation than the present group of younger women expressing themselves through the various dimensions of women's liberation, I have been more willing to take my time. I did not even have available to me conceptual categories to be helpful in assessing my role as woman in the church, and have again and again had to experience myself as "outsider," woman who needed to "prove herself," woman separated from her sisters by being told "but, Peggy, you are different." What I am saying is that I don't understand myself as an expression of the church's concern about women, but much more of an historical accident. Thus I do not sense the existence of a supportive system for my sisters and myself that we should choose to claim as authorizing our ministries.

Certainly it is a legitimate question to ask me why I stick with it. Insofar as my role on the faculty of the Divinity School of the University of Chicago is concerned, I experience myself as minister much more than as administrator, which is half of my appointment, or as teacher, which is the other half. I understand that my primary ministerial functions occur wherever I am. I also consider the Divinity School very fortunate to have me on its faculty, rather than myself being honored by my presence here. It is important for women to learn how to make such statements. So many of us, inside and outside the churches, accept our privileges as philanthropic gifts granted to unworthy slaves. We then do not question the broader issues or fall into the even more unfortunate trap of assuming, "Well, I made it, so can my sisters." Thus I refuse ultimately to celebrate my appointment here because I am once again an accident, an intrusion, separated from my sisters and hence, in a real sense alone, and quite aware that my appointment does not necessarily speak to the deeper issues about women in the church with which we must be dealing.

It is important to me that I celebrate my experience of freedom to choose. In a real sense, my jobs within the church have been sacrifices. It is not pleasant always to be the first, to be alone and without a support system, to be having to sort out those aspects of the masculine consciousness which affect myself and my sisters. Nor, with my background, is it pleasant to be continually experiencing the failures of the men in the church to carry out their tasks at the same time as they deny my sisters responsibilities because they are unqualified, of the wrong emotional disposition, or otherwise unable to participate. My own experiences indicate to me that there are real limitations in the masculine consciousness which have not been conceptualized and that many of the church's "failures" are closely related to problems with masculine identity which are so "self-evident" that ways to deal with them do not even exist.

Thus choice is of vital importance to me; I choose to be wherever I am in relation to "the church it" and do not allow "it" to control me or to use me to point untruthfully about its openness to respond to women who choose ministry. I am choosing, *and I choose every day,* to be on this faculty, and I frequently come very close to saying "No."

Let me add what I have suggested earlier—I find no real differences in my experiences as a woman in the church whether I am relating to "conservatives," "liberals," or "radicals." The masculine consciousness appears to be the primary ordering principle, rather than any particular polity or political persuasion. It helps to remember that the original thrust of women's liberation came out of student radicals who discovered that women's role in the radical movement was as limited to secretarial tasks as it was in more conservative masculine undertakings. I have found no correlation between where a man stands on church renewal or the church's role in the world and where he stands on the role of women in church and society. This has been deceptive and disappointing for many women who have made another assumption. To quote from Simon and Garfunkel: "O my grace, there ain't no hiding place."

I am also still choosing to be present amidst the structures because even a modest presence is a reminder to men and women alike of the turbulent issues that underlie my being there. It is particularly important to women struggling with questions of vocation to have some real live "identity models" in relation to which they can come to terms with their own decisions. I also feel a responsibility to be where I can stimulate concern and thought as to what ministries with women might be. Whether we look at our "conservatives" or our "experimenters" we find almost a complete vacuum of understandings about feminine experience, needs and possibilities. Our seminaries may admit women, but they have not considered it necessary to have any feminine presence, existentially or conceptually. The 56 per cent of women occupying the pews of the

Presbyterian Church and the 60 per cent in the Baptist Church have not experienced any of the benefits of thinking about pastoral counseling directly related to the real problems and questions which are part of women's lives. There has been no attempt to reach out to secular women, to discover who they are and what the nature of their existence is in an exploding world, although we have done this with minority groups and others who have forced us to take them seriously. We are so obvious in our numbers that we are not even noticed, and so taken for granted that we refuse to raise up questions about ourselves. At the same time we send young men off into parishes, experimental ministries or social action endeavors without any grounding or understanding of the women with whom they will be working. There is a strong anti-intellectual trend here; we assume that any order of relationship with wife or girl friend qualifies one to minister with women. It is not at all surprising that pastors step back from this role, keep women in their women's society enclaves, almost without exception give black men preferential treatment, and fail to initiate creative scholarship or ministries that have anything at all to do with us. I would be less than honest not to state directly that I consider the Missouri Synod syndrome to be the controlling factor in the way in which the church relates to me and my sisters.

I have suggested earlier that all is not well among our masculine controlled bureaucracies and decision-making structures, and I also consider it highly important that I do not "become like them" in my process of working out my own understandings of ministry. I will save development of this thought for another time; but the degree of confinement by myth and culture among men in the church is frightening to me, and I experience an almost complete lack of free men among the creators of the present church. From this comes some of my affirmation that the church needs the sisters; the separation of whatever we may eventually define as the masculine and feminine consciousness can only do disservice to our commitments and ministries.

Thus, as I stated in a sermon earlier this year, "I will call you brother even though you will not call me sister." I will reach out to you even though you will not reach out to me. I will affirm our mutuality as persons seeking to make a common witness even though you are not free to do so. Here I will insist on being highly theological even though you are culture-bound.

I cannot accept the structures as the authorization of my ministry. If that were all I had, I would be an empty human and minister indeed.

An Authority of Possibility

I consider the authority of my ministry to be rooted in the authority of possibility. I am delighted at this point of my life that I don't have any safety or niches in Scripture or in history or in myth or in structures; I am delighted in my present understanding that the authority of my ministry is rooted in futures and in possibilities, and in a Faith experienced so profoundly that "nothing in all Creation shall separate me from the love of God which is in Christ Jesus our Lord . . ." not even Scripture, or history, or myth, or structure, or the masculine consciousness.

I once ended a sermon on this subject with the constructive statement: "I will cry unto my God—let us free one another!" A part of the authority of my ministry lies in the possibility of freeing God from the types of abuse which keeps God bound to a masculine hermeneutic, history and grammatical structure. And because the authority of my ministry is essentially rooted in my own religious experience as it has intersected with Scripture, history, myth, the church, cultural analysis and people experiences, I consider myself to be a freer servant than many of my masculine colleagues.

In this period of history it is vitally important for a woman, especially a woman moving in a masculine world and in a masculine profession made up of contemporary patristic fathers, to have trust in herself as an actualizing human person who is self-identified, free to choose, free to select that to which or to whom she will be responsible, and free to choose to bow down before God. I cannot bow down before a God who will not first let me stand up. I understand that much of the scriptural and theological-historical tradition places me in a position where it is very difficult to bow down as a full human being (and hence to give the act of bowing ultimate significance). In the various myths about the nature of feminine existence, my bowing down becomes a matter of form rather than of Faith, a matter of unquestioning acceptance of a cultural role validated in religious terminology, rather than a personal statement of me as a person-of-Faith who is struggling with doubt and affirmation, with the nature of relationships and of structures, with the meanings and absurdities of human existence.

Moreover, as a woman self-consciously experiences the processes of her own liberation and its implications for ministry, the possibilities of contributing to the church's understandings of the nature of freedom and possibility, liberation processes and ministerial roles in relation to them open up for serious discussion. In a world in which the church has had to deal with a variety of peoples-in-process-of-liberation, some conceptual material could be helpful indeed, as well as enhancing to a sense of ministry as possibility.

Women appear to go through certain stages of becoming liberated, including early ambivalence marked by curiosity and suspicion (it is painful and fearful to grasp Freedom!); developing feelings of anger and hostility as they realize the forces hampering their own development toward personhood; experiences of celebration and, almost, ecstasy as possibilities and options become rooted within them; and a real freeing of energies to be creatively about the exploration of possibilities. There is little in the literature that has explored such dynamics, and almost no help offered to persons caught up in the processes, whether they are moving toward liberation or are seen to be—and usually realistically are—standing in the way. For the church to take on the felt experiences of real human struggles is to me one of the real possibilities which authorizes my ministry.

There is another factor. Those many groups who have been experiencing the need for and the reality of liberation, have an assortment of experiences with human existence and structures that moves them closely toward the possibility of grasping the absurdities of the Christian Faith, particularly as symbolically expressed in categories having to do with Crucifixion and Resurrection. I am speaking of blacks and browns, the gay community, reds, the poor, women and others—and I am not speaking naively, sentimentally or one-dimensionally. I am suggesting only that there are orders of present human experiences which are so pregnant with possibility that my ministry can be validated as one of possibility and futures.

Thus a very real sense of possibility and futures intrudes itself upon a church so often caught up in despair and the past. For I am talking about a process of human growth and development that includes within it—with full integrity—the recognition of the utter sinfulness of its structures and the depths of its despair from having been at the limits of human finitude, and somehow also, the recognition through the processes of liberation, that it still has something to affirm—in spite of and because of. With church and world in such desperate need of the affirmation of possibilities and futures, such deep groundings in experiences that are real rather than rhetorical, worthwhile rather than popular, have much to offer. "What is worthwhile?" becomes the question-cry of my students; can the masculine consciousness possibly cope?

I also find my ministry to be authorized by those persons with whom I minister. I do not understand myself as completely departing from the tendency of masculine theologians to sneak in personal experience to validate their conceptualizations. In fact, I understand myself as beginning to make demands to be viewed with the Pauls and the Luthers, the Tillichs and the Niebuhrs, the Ogdens and the Gilkeys, who have not had to claim their sexual right to be conceptualizers of the Faith in order to function in such roles. It is part of the feminine self-image not to make such claims and not to conceptualize our own integral experiences and intellectualizings of the Faith. Hence I feel free to depart from the tradition and to question—to affirm possibilities with which I have hardly begun to deal—to have felt suggestions which I cannot begin to conceptualize—and always to test out those self-evidents with which the masculine consciousness has penetrated me.

For to me it is very real to be validated and authorized by those persons with whom I minister, my students, my sisters along the full continuum of women's liberation, my black friends, the gay community—and, for me, the parish ministers with whom I share so much, the women who stay home and raise their children and look to their husbands for identity, denominational executives and even my colleagues on the faculty. For certainly a part of my felt authority comes from experiences which I share with the persons with whom I seek to enter into the meaning of human existence, and their challenges to me as to how it is to be conceptualized and how they are to move toward a sense of full and rooted humanity.

As I do these things—examine the process and the experience; test out the guiding values, principles and traditions which affect them; discern and disclose myths; experience the possibilities of new creations of persons, institutions and cultures—as I do these things, I *experience* the authority of what I am calling possibility, the authority of a God of possibility, a God who is utterly absurd and utterly real and of worth in the type of world in which we live. For this I need biblical, historical and ecclesiastical perspectives, along with a vast assortment of cultural understandings and principles, but for this I do not need any other authorities than those suggested above.

And as my students get caught up in the authority of possibility, they do not need to be threatened by the authority of Scriptures and tradition, but can freely turn to them to find what is offered to us. As my students experience possibilities and futures, human finitude and doubt, they can turn freely to history to seek further understanding of what is of lasting worth. And as my students and I grasp a sense of our own worth, there is less necessity of being "like others" and more real openness to engagement in the processes of seeking truth and meaning. "Self-evidents" are less binding, and new creations can be experienced.

A passion for incarnation is a driving force within me, and I know of no other way to grasp it than by experience intersected always by a variety of conceptualizations. This, for me, means an authority of ministry coming from Presence, Process Participation, Principle Clarification, and Possibility. Perhaps it is ironic to view myself as standing closely with Paul, for "neither life nor death, nor powers nor principalities, nor things in the heavens above or the earth beneath . . ." nor Scripture, nor history, nor denominations, nor culture, nor the pervasiveness of the masculine consciousness . . . shall keep *me* from the love of God who is Christ Jesus our Lord and who is the only One who can authorize my ministry.

NOTES

1. *The Springfielder*, March 1970.
2. Barbara Buggert Lane, "The Woman's Century," unpublished paper for a Church History course at the University of Chicago Divinity School.

APPENDIX

It is clear from the preceding chapters, that the movement for the liberation of women in the church has only begun and will continue as an ongoing process for many years. At such a point in the history of a movement the clearest picture of its aspirations and goals is often to be found in the documents, resolutions and position papers of the groups involved. What follows is an abbreviated attempt to cover the wide realm of activity in the church at the present and to portray the diversity of opinions, strategies and demands which are encompassed in the movement. Hopefully these will not only serve as reference materials but will also convey the many-sided nature of this attempt by women to make meaningful changes in the life of the church.

A.   Detroit 1969

During the past two years, women in various denominations and church bodies have formed distinct groups, often called caucuses, which are composed solely of women and which have as their main purpose the increased participation of women in a meaningful way in the life of their particular organization. Just as youths, blacks and other minority groups have found this a useful tactic for achieving their goals, women found they had more strength and more influence when they worked together in caucuses. More important, they experienced a new sense of unity and fellowship in working together in their own causes.

The caucus which received earliest attention was formed at the General Assembly of the National Council of Churches of Christ which was held at Detroit in December of 1969. The statement of this caucus was one of the first examples of a new consciousness and solidarity among women in the church.

THE GROUP

We are an informal group. We are members of churches represented here. Some of us are voting delegates, either by membership in the General Assembly or by substitution. The statement that is to follow is not unanimously consented to in every part by those who are standing, but it is a consensus of the group.

THE STATEMENT

We begin our statement with an affirmation of support for the movement to liberate women in the United States. This movement is a part of the spirit of the '60's which will continue, because it is raising crucial issues and pointing to new possibilities for humanity and especially for that portion of humanity which has chosen to gather into *the church*. Women's oppression and woman's liberation is a basic part of the struggle of blacks, browns, youth, and others. We will not be able to create a new church and a new society until and unless women are full participants. We intend to be full participants.

Many who are seated here may be unaware of the unrest that is growing among thinking women, an unrest that is finding expression in formally organized fashion across the country. In many publications, ranging all the way from avant garde to household magazines, this theme is sounded, that the women of this country are gathering themselves into a sweat of civil revolt, and the general population seems totally unaware of what is happening; or, indeed, that anything is happening; or that there is a legitimate need behind what is happening. How is this possible? Why is it true? What relation is there between the peculiarly unalarmed, amused dismissal of the women's rights movement and the movement itself? Is this relation only coincidental, only the generally apathetic response of a society already benumbed by civil rights and student anarchy and unable to rise to yet one more protest movement, or is it more to the point in the case of women's rights; is it not, in fact, precisely the key to the entire issue?

But even on economic grounds or grounds of legal discrimination most people are dismally ignorant of the true proportions of the issue. . . . This is closer to the facts:

Women in this country make 60 cents for every $1 a man makes.

Women do not share in the benefits of the fair employment practices laws because those laws do not specify "no discrimination on the basis of sex."

Women often rise in salary only to the point at which a man starts.

Women occupy, in great masses, the "household tasks" of industry. They are nurses but not doctors, secretaries but not executives, researchers but not writers, workers but not managers, bookkeepers but not promoters.

Women almost never occupy decision- or policy-making positions.

Women are almost nonexistent in government.

Women are subject to a set of "protective" laws that restrict their working hours, do not allow them to occupy many jobs in which the carrying of weights is involved, do not allow them to enter innumerable bars, restaurants, hotels, and other public places unescorted.

"The woman's issue is the true barometer of social change," said a famous political theoretician. This was true 100 years ago; it is no less true today. Women and blacks were and are, traditionally and perpetually, the great "outsiders" in Western culture, and their erratic swellings of outrage parallel each other in a number of ways that are both understandable and also extraordinary.

When we look back into history, we know as well as blacks know that "we've been here before." We've experienced change up to a certain point, only to fall back. We are now serving notice, and if we do not, others will, *that we will finish the job this time.*

We want you to recognize that when we talk about woman's liberation in the life of the church we are thinking about what is going on in the Roman Catholic church as well as in Protestant and Orthodox churches, that we are talking about what is happening to women in the black churches as well as in the predominantly white churches.

So women are rising; that is our first point. We are rising, black and white, red and brown, to demand change, to demand humanity for ourselves as well as for others. You will be hearing from us in the '70's. You will be hearing from us because this holism is basic to our concept of the nature of the church, and of the church's mission in the '70's. You cannot seriously undertake the quest for meaning and wholeness called for in the Mission in the '70's Report unless you are willing to deal with the role of women. "Search for community in a modern secular society" will be futile if we do not now face up to what it means that God created human life in *"our* image—male and female."

Secondly, we wish to present some facts which illustrate the situation of women. Nowhere is the situation of women better illustrated than in our male-dominated and male-oriented churches. The church, both in its theology and in its institutional forms, is a reflection of culture. It has shown no propensity to transcend culture as regards the status of women, although it knows that it ought. Indeed, the church has too often maintained anachronistic attitudes and practices long after other societal institutions have begun to shift.

Let us look at certain statistics regarding the NCC itself. In 1950 when the NCC was organized in Cleveland, Ohio, only 5 out of 82 members of the General Board were women. That was 6 per cent. Twenty-four churches out of 29, or approximately 82 per cent, had no women in their delegations.

Nineteen years later in 1969, out of approximately 200 members of the General Board, 11—or barely 6 per cent—are women. Out of a total of 786 official delegates in the General Assembly, 95 are women. That is 12.1 per cent of the total. There are still 13 denominations out of 33 in the council's membership—or 40 per cent—which have no women delegates.

Were a visitor from outer space to visit the Assembly and were that visitor told that it was a body representative of the churches in the United States, that visitor would naturally conclude that the churches are composed of white-skinned male clergy over 40. We know how far from the truth that assumption would be, for, we repeat, we are in the churches.

It is not only in the composition of the Assembly, which we know is a creature of the denominations and only reflects the denomination's inattention to its female membership. We also see this bias reflected in the appointments that have come forth from the Nominating Committee. It is reflected in the committees into which the Assembly has organized itself for this week and on into the next triennium. The total number of women delegates for the next triennium is now 95, the same as this past triennium. The total in the General Board is only 18, which is one less than at present.

An analysis of the representation at the General Assembly shows that women were distinctly in the minority. Despite the fact that a substantial portion of the church's membership (certainly over 50 per cent) is women, they were not represented in Detroit. The action of the women in caucusing and declaring their support for the movement to liberate women was thus highly significant and represented the first occasion where the women of the National Council of Churches declared themselves openly, in the very presence of the overwhelmingly male-dominated organized church.

PERCENTAGE OF WOMEN DELEGATES TO NCC ASSEMBLY

Denomination *	Total delegates	Women	% Women
Philadelphia Yearly Meeting of the Religious Society of Friends	7	3	42.9
American Baptist Convention	35	10	28.3
United Church of Christ	43	11	25.6
United Presbyterian Church in the U.S.A.	58	13	22.4
Episcopal Church	45	9	20
Christian Church (Disciples)	37	7	18.9
Christian Methodist Episcopal	15	2	15.3
Friends United Meeting	9	1	11
Lutheran Church in America	37	4	10.8
Polish National Catholic Church of America	10	1	10
Presbyterian Church in the U.S.	20	2	10
United Methodist Church	182	17	9.3
Reformed Church in America	11	1	9.2
Greek Orthodox Archdiocese of North and South America	31	2	6.5
National Baptist Convention of America	43	2	4.6
Syrian (Orthodox) Church of Antioch	7	3	4.3
African Methodist Episcopal Church	24	1	4.2
African Methodist Episcopal Zion Church	20	4	2
National Baptist Convention, U.S.A., Inc.	55	1	1.8
Seventh Day Baptist General Conference	7	1	1.5
TOTAL	786	95	12.1

* 13 denominations had no women delegates.

We offer another set of statistics. In a survey of employment of women in professional or executive positions in the churches at the national level conducted earlier this year, 65 national religious agencies related to 17 denominations and the NCC were polled on salary scales and other practices.

The survey revealed that the proportion of men to women is much higher for all salary grades above $12,500. The modal grade for men (34.5 per cent) is from $12,500 to $15,000, while for women the modal grade (39.1 per cent) is *two steps down,* from $7,500 to $10,000.

In summary, these data reflected adherence to the rhetoric of equality of opportunity for women and men, on the one hand, and the factual conditions of considerable discrimination on the other.

Many times, evidence such as the above is turned aside by the reminder that, after all, women do comprise a numerical majority in the churches, and even in certain situations, due to women's pattern of attendance, we comprise healthy majorities. It is up to us to begin to exercise the prerogatives of such phenomena. We must do this.

Now, what are our future plans? Generally speaking, we have just begun to find a coherent voice and to organize ourselves. We are not really organized in this Assembly. But it will happen all throughout the churches, in local congregations, at the national level, and in the World Council of Churches. There are obstacles, not least among them, many women themselves. We women have our Aunt Janes even if we do not have our Uncle Toms.

Secondly, with regard to this Assembly and to the next triennium, as the Council is called to re-examine functions and roles, indeed the very nature of the church in mission, it simply must deal with women. You will be sick of this theme, but we will not stop raising it. Indeed, we cannot. And we cannot wait for the silent majority of women to find their voice. The new creature that will be created in and amongst the churches must be born of the efforts of the whole church.

We join in the demand voiced from many quarters for change to permit full participation of the laity—for women and men laity, for young people, for working-class people and the poor, for all minorities.

We will not desert a single cause to which we have devoted ourselves in the past. We only ask our allies to support our cause, and that we not repeat the mistakes of the past that left all women behind at times of great social change. All the various quests for justice to which this body is committed are inextricably linked. That is the lesson of history. After the Civil War, when so many women worked for Abolition, the franchise was granted only to black males, and it took women, black and white, another 60 years to get the vote. In making these assertions, we want you to know that we know that many assembled here, out of deep theological conviction regarding the nature of the church and the nature of humanity, share our concern and support our cause.

Now with regard to this Assembly and the elections which will take place, we must point out the paucity of women nominees. You can expect that an effort will be made at the appropriate time to correct what is to us a sad situation. We know there are many among us who are qualified to serve; placing our considerable economic resources at the disposal of the church, many have been disillusioned by the experience of being categorized only as interpreters and fund-raisers.

We will also direct our attention to the working sections, and to the resolutions which will issue from this body.

In conclusion, we reiterate our support for the effort to liberate women. We announce to this Assembly that women are on the move, and, using a current phrase, we make the prediction that "the next great movement in history" will be ours.

B.   **Statement—Women's Caucus**

Following the example of the women at Detroit, denominational women formed caucuses at the annual meeting of their churches or at their conference meetings. An example is this statement from the Women's Caucus of the Massachusetts Conference of the United Church of Christ.

The Women's Caucus began early in 1970 when a small group of United Church of Christ women from Massachusetts gathered at Framingham Conference Center to discuss the Women's Revolution. We originated as an ad hoc committee and have essentially remained that.

As Christian women we believe it is important that women become more deeply involved in the significant decision-making processes of our Church and society. We recognize and affirm the current movement for women's liberation, and see ourselves as part of it, with our primary responsibility being to work for change in church structures and theology so as to provide for greater freedom for women throughout all of our society.

For this reason and others we have put forward three resolutions at the 1970 Annual Meeting of the Mass. Conference: on Freedom of Choice Concerning Abortion, Sex Education, and Family Planning. We have also initiated some proposed bylaw changes which work directly to maximize the involvement of women at policy-making levels of the Conference. One bylaw change will eradicate references to a cleric as "the man," in view of the fact that the U.C.C. ordains women to the ministry.

In addition, a special room at the Annual Meeting has been set aside as "The Woman's Place" where women can gather to discuss issues and topics of mutual concern. The room is located at The Hatch in the cafeteria of the Student Union. A variety of literature relating to all aspects of the movement for women's rights is available, as are refreshments and a graphic display.

We invite all interested women to join us.

THE WOMEN'S CAUCUS

C.   Resolution—Diocese of Central New York
of the Protestant Episcopal Church

*The demands of women's caucuses have been received in various
ways by denominational bodies. This resolution by the Central New
York Diocese of the Episcopal Church is an example of a specific response which ranges from questions of language in church services and
constitutions to equal employment and participation in the church.*

Resolved, That the Diocese of Central New York present the following memorials to the General Convention of the Episcopal Church
at Houston:

Whereas, discrimination based on sex is destructive of religious values, and

Whereas, certain canons of the Episcopal Church appear to re-enforce
such discrimination, therefore, be it

Resolved, That wherever the words *he, him, his,* are used in the Constitution and Canons of the Protestant Episcopal Church, there be
added the words *she, her, hers.*

Whereas, discrimination based on sex is destructive of religious values, whereas certain sections of the Book of Common Prayer appear to
re-enforce such discrimination, therefore, be it

Resolved, That the response of the woman in the marriage ceremony
in the Book of Common Prayer be rewritten; "I plight thee my troth"
and that the "Thanksgiving of Women after Childbirth" be either
deleted or revised to read, "The Thanksgiving of Parents after Childbirth," commonly called "The Churching of Parents," and the rite be
rewritten accordingly.

Whereas, discrimination based on sex is destructive of religious values, therefore, be it

Resolved, That every diocese and every parish be encouraged to include full representation of women as well as men on vestries, diocesan
boards and committees.

Whereas, discrimination based on sex is destructive of religious values, therefore, be it

Resolved, That all church institutions, educational and other, be immediately desegregated to encourage full representation of women as well
as men on boards of trustees, on faculties and in the student bodies of
such church-supported institutions.

(Upon motion of the Committee, duly seconded, this resolution was
carried.)

D.   Resolution—American Baptist Convention

Some denominations, for example the United Presbyterian Church in the USA and the American Baptist Convention, have begun far-reaching plans for action in response to the varied demands of women. This resolution concerning increased opportunities for women was adopted by the Baptists at their annual meeting in Seattle in May of 1969. While specific means of implementing the proposals are not given, the document does demonstrate denominational awareness of the multi-level nature of the discrimination which women face in the church and in society.

Since our Christian faith affirms the dignity and worth of every individual, Christians bear the responsibility to achieve their potential and to participate fully in society according to their ability and desires;

And since the American Baptist Convention has been appointing fewer women to advanced decision-making positions in recent years, a great loss of perspective and leadership has been suffered by the Convention as individuals of ability have not been discovered or utilized;

And since there has been a significant decline (50 per cent in the last five years) of the number of women on state convention professional staff, there is little opportunity for women to have executive staff experience;

And since the few women who serve as pastors find themselves limited to a few states with very few choices as to the types of churches served; and since the number of women serving as ministers or directors of Christian Education has been steadily declining; and since the pay scale for women who are pastors or directors of Christian Education has been low with little hope of improvement,

Many women in church-related vocations have ceased to encourage young women to prepare themselves for such service while others have left or are considering leaving their church-related vocations; and since the American Baptist Convention needs leadership and cannot afford to underutilize the talent and ability of women.

We urge the American Baptist Convention and its affiliated organizations and constituent churches to—

1. Reverse the declining number of positions held by professionally trained women in local churches, states, cities and regional and national staffs by—

    a. Examining their assumptions, practices and policies which have contributed to the decrease in the number of women entering or continuing in church-related vocations;

   b. Recognizing that the traditional mode of thought concerning church occupations has been primarily male in orientation and encouraging young women to prepare themselves to enter all church-related vocations and insisting on a greater acceptance of women in roles traditionally restricted to men;

   c. Eliminating inequalities in compensation;

   d. Re-examining the training and promotion practices to provide opportunities for women to fill more top level jobs;

   e. Initiating new assistance to women pastors for placement opportunities in a wider variety of churches;

   f. Conserving trained women who may, for various reasons (marriage, young children, etc.) temporarily leave church-related vocations. We recommend that the Board of Education and Publication explore possible programs for continuing education appropriate to their needs.

2. Establish policies and practices in electing and appointing persons to offices, committees and boards to ensure more adequate opportunities for women.

3. Urge member churches to give equal status to women in positions of major responsibility (deacons, moderators, trustees, etc.) within the local church.

And since women in our society suffer discrimination in the political and economic as well as the religious life of our country and are not recruited for professional and managerial training and often find themselves passed over for promotions,

We also urge that:

1. Title VII of the Civil Rights Act of 1964 which "prohibits discrimination in employment on the basis of sex" be strictly enforced;

2. Political parties re-examine their practices with a view to the greater participation of women at policy-making levels;

3. Women be encouraged to seek public office and voters consider candidates on the basis of qualification without regard to sex;

4. Industry, government and the professions avoid tokenism and open more top-level jobs to women, giving greater attention to staff development and promotion;

5. Women be allowed and encouraged to seek fulfillment and service to their community as they resume their education or training for or participation in various professional or nonprofessional occupations during later periods of their lives;

6. A careful re-evaluation of job classification be undertaken to make certain that men and women receive equal pay for equal work.

E.   Statement—Women's Division of Board of Missions, United Methodist Church

Many women's divisions and women's units in various denominations have been under pressure from structure committees to disband and be incorporated into other bodies. Some groups have decided on their own that they no longer want to be "special interest" groups, and that they can achieve fuller participation in the life of their own church if they disband. However, other women at the highest level of the organized church have begun to sense that "their time has come" and they follow the "separatist" example of the caucus in strongly urging women to stay together and work for themselves as well as for the larger church. The statement of the Women's Division of the Board of Missions of the United Methodist Church to the structure committee of the church contains many of the justifications for separate women's organizations at this point in history.

COLLABORATION, COALITION, COMMITMENT

For the Women's Division 1969 has been a trial year. It has been tried and proved faithful in an effort to unite the best of two former groups. Joint planning in 1968 has made it possible to concentrate on common tasks. A nationwide constituency of 1,976,597 has taken the lead in working through details of merger.

Increasing efforts are made within the Board of Missions, of which the Women's Division is part, to facilitate the decision-making process within and between its several units. This has not been easy, since each unit has a peculiar responsibility. Nowhere does this element of peculiarity manifest itself more than in the Women's Division. It is the only unit:

—which has a lay constituency;

—which has administrative, interpretive and educational functions; and which makes financial appropriations to all units (except UMCOR) of the Board.

So collaboration takes on a new meaning as the Women's Division gets involved in understanding the programs of other units and, through participation of Board members, helps make decisions in those units.

Implicit in the collaborative style is testing ideas and programs against views of others which can eventuate in more meaningful ideas and programs. Collaboration must protect the freedom and flexibility of each unit to perform its unique tasks without damaging the whole.

Coalition has become the style of work for those who need others of like mind to cope with current issues. The Women's Division has, through its predecessor groups, always been in coalition with other church women's groups in mutual support of programs.

It is necessary to extend these coalitions to include nontraditional groups such as National Welfare Rights Organization, a contemporary organizational phenomenon, and the younger women's liberation groups. Coalition with the latter is still in development stages. As the issue of women's role, assigned by church and society, comes into greater conflict with desire for personhood and participation in the whole of life, a strengthened coalition is imperative.

Commitment is what the Women's Division is all about. Part of its *Purpose* states ". . . to develop a personal responsibility for the whole task of the church."

As a result of probing by its Long-Range Planning and Policy Commitees, the Women's Division in its 1969 Spring Meeting adopted the following statement for presentation to the General Conference Commission on Structure:

1. The Women's Division has as its first concern the renewal of the church and the strengthening and sustaining of its mission in the world.

2. The church is entering an era of dispersion, which to us means at least the following:

    a. Definition of the mission of the church (defining its works and deciding how to do it) is increasingly localized.

    b. Individual members are becoming less attached to forms and activities associated with the traditional church.

3. Structures are needed which can be partially characterized as:

    a. A network of mutual support (horizontal) as opposed to a system of giving, of responding to programs or directives (vertical).

    b. A system of communication that is quickly and easily grasped, conveying useful resources, preventing provincialism.

    c. A style of action which is flexible and provisional enough for ready response to emerging needs and crises.

    d. A missional stance that frees rather than absorbs resources, that loosens rather than bridles creative power, that energizes persons rather than sapping their energies for maintaining purposes.

4. The church is experienced in two forms:

    a. The traditional, institutional church, which step by painful step is being modified and is shifting priorities in a more or less systematic fashion. Such a church is historical and societal. Such a church is evolutionary.

    b. The church that is "beyond the church," drawing together

those Christians who do not find it necessary to call themselves by any name, i.e., Protestant or Catholic. This church is "post-denominational," even "post-ecumenical," having already gone beyond the Vatican II and COCU. This church is biblical. It is revolutionary.

5. In tension with the reality of both, each is searching for new forms of service and witness, significant changes in values, styles of life and ways of thinking and feeling about the world.

6. Structures which are open ended, fluid, provisional, flexible will have the most significant impact upon values, life style and modes of thought and feeling. We believe the reflection action style (the unity of spiritual life and social action) is the characteristic mode of persons participating in such structures.

7. If the Division's predecessors left any legacy, it is that the Women's Division now offers to the church an unfragmented structure which historically and presently witnesses to the unity of reflection and action as the essence of mission.

8. Can exercising this mission best be done by losing ourselves or by maintaining our visibility for the foreseeable future?

9. For the church to be obedient in the whole of its life and work, it is essential that all participate in "the laos."

10. The present structures of society, including especially ecclesiastical structures, are male oriented. It is not easy for women to participate.

11. Within the Board of Missions (and in co-operation with other agencies) women through organization have found meaningful opportunities for service; and they have contributed to the growth and maturity of the Boards toward the aim of renewal of the church.

12. Where organized women's groups have been removed from a visible policy-making and power-sharing role, the following things tend to occur:

   a. Male chauvinism increases;

   b. The status of women declines;

   c. The image of "the laos" is distorted.

13. For the sake of the whole, as well as for ourselves, we believe that our denomination needs to maintain an organized women's group which exercises real power. Otherwise, women will have to reorganize later under more difficult circumstances.

14. Women want to be catalysts for the continued humanization of God's world, mobilizers of the resources of women, creators of new arenas for their participation throughout the church and world, and in coalition with other women't groups, with youth and with people of color, to be reconcilers in all the rough places.

15. The Women's Division represents only that segment of United Methodist women who have organized to support and participate in mission. Women have found themselves in the missionary outreach of the church and wish to remain within whatever structure carries forward that mandate.

F.   Resolutions—General Division of Women's Work
           32nd Triennial Meeting Protestant Episcopal Church

The Methodist statement represents a distinctive new thrust in the ongoing discussion of the representation of women in the church. Other denominations have not necessarily followed the same course of reasoning. In 1967 the General Division of Women's Work of the Episcopal Church at the triennial meeting of that church took the position that their programs should be integrated into other structures within the church. The following statement on the restructuring of the Division explains this decision.

Whereas the 1964 Resolution on Critical Analysis of Organizational Structure has resulted in the discovery that the General Division of Women's Work cannot restructure unrelated to the Executive Council; and

Whereas together with other departments and units the General Division has planned jointly the program objectives for the coming triennium; and

Whereas freedom to experiment with new structures and methods is necessary to enable fresh responses to our changing imperatives: Now, therefore, be it

Resolved, That the General Division of Women's Work and its committees be encouraged to enter into such new structures, in connection with other departments and units of the Executive Council, as seem appropriate to discharge the responsibilities and functions now vested in the Division and/or the respective units.

(Adopted by 32nd Triennial Meeting, Seattle, Washington, September 21, 1967.)

Significantly, the Episcopal women also felt that the representation of women as a specific portion of the church's constituency was no longer a priority. Note the suggestion that a periodic assembly would be composed of "persons who would represent the church, not just the women of the church."

Whereas the Triennial Meeting has become a tradition which yields great benefits to those who attend: information, education, inspiration for the women of the church; and

Whereas the Bylaws of the Triennial Meeting describe, in Section 2 of Article I, the delegates as representatives of "the *women* of the diocese/district/convocation"; and

Whereas the structures of the Episcopal Church women's organizations are being reorganized in many dioceses and abolished in some, making further participation of their delegates in a Triennial Meeting, as representatives "of the women," a debatable matter; and

Whereas a Triennial Meeting, or a periodic assembly, made up of delegates who would be recruited from those persons, men and women, whose primary responsibility is for the education and communication of the Church's whole program to all the persons in the diocese/district, could yield great benefits to the Church at every level: Now, therefore, be it

Resolved, That it is the sense of this Triennial Meeting that the General Division of Women's Work, under the authority granted it in Article V, Section 4 of the Bylaws, seriously consider a periodic assembly made up of persons who would represent the Church, not just the women of the Church; and that such an assembly be planned in co-operation with other units of the Executive Council; and be it further

Resolved, That an assembly be held at the same time and place as General Convention in order to discuss in depth current major issues facing the Church.

(Adopted by 32nd Triennial Meeting, Seattle, Washington, Sept. 22, 1967)

G.   Graymoor Resolution

The actions of the 1967 assembly were to be effected by 1970. In the intervening years, however, it became obvious to many women that it was more important than ever to ensure the representation and participation of women in the church. In contrast to the preceding position, this statement from a group of Episcopal women indicates the increasing insistence of younger and more militant women that denominational bodies respond to the needs and demands of women.

The institutional Episcopal Church is racist, militaristic, and sexist; its basic influence on our own lives is negative. The Church is not living the Gospel in our lives and in the world today.

Whereas any discrimination within the Episcopal Church is antithetical to the teachings of Jesus Christ and is destructive of Christian values; and

Whereas, when such discrimination affects not only minority groups but also oppresses more than half of the membership of the Church, namely women, the very existence of the Church as the Body of Christ is threatened; and

Whereas neither man nor woman can be a whole human being as long as either man or woman exploits or is exploited by another; and

Whereas it is the obligation of the existing hierarchy of the Church to assert leadership in finding ways of implementing their principles; and

Whereas, moreover, the Church has taught, but rarely believed in, the concept of the priesthood of the laity: Therefore be it

Resolved, That women as well as men be accepted and recognized as equals so that they may function in proportion to their numbers in all aspects of the Church's life and ministry, including, but not limited to:

a. parish committees and guilds, vestries, cathedral chapters, diocesan councils, standing committees, diocesan officers, provincial synods, General Conventions, Executive Council, and joint commissions, such as liturgical and budgetary, etc.,

b. Bishops, priests, deacons, postulants, candidates for Holy Orders, examining chaplains, licensed lay readers with privilege of the Chalice, subdeacons, acolytes, crucifers, thurifers, and ushers, and

c. seminary faculty, administrators and trustees; other educational personnel; institutional ministries and chaplaincies; and be it further

Resolved, That the Church shall take positive action to remedy the historical discrimination against women and its destructive effects upon the Christian community, by

a. the immediate ordination of those women graduates of our seminaries who desire ordination and also of those religious women who have college or equivalent education,
b. open admissions to all seminaries,
c. special recruitment and scholarship aid for women applicants to seminaries,
d. equal opportunities for employment within the Church in accordance with national standards set forth in Title VII of the Civil Rights Act of 1964 and the Equal Pay Act of 1963,
e. education of congregations to the mutual responsibility and interdependence of persons as members of the Body of Christ.

(This resolution formulated by a group of Concerned Women gathered together at the Franciscan Retreat House of Graymoor, Garrison, N. Y., on April 24–26, 1970.)

H. Employment of Women

There seems to be good evidence to support the assertion that women are not now participating on an equal basis in church work. The following study supports the contention of women that they do indeed encounter discrimination at the top levels of the church. This study was first presented as a paper at a Consultation on the Recruiting, Training and Employing of Women Professional Church Workers held at Seabury House, Greenwich, Connecticut, on February 26 and 27, 1969. The consultation was sponsored by Church Women United and the women executives of the Churches.

A STUDY OF EMPLOYMENT OF WOMEN IN PROFESSIONAL OR EXECUTIVE POSITIONS IN THE CHURCHES AT A NATIONAL LEVEL

by Earl D. C. Brewer, Ph.D.

Director, Department of Research, National Council of Churches

This study reviews descriptive data tabulated from responses to a questionnaire mailed to 156 national denominational boards and agencies. Responses were received from 65 boards and agencies related to 17 denominations and the National Council of Churches. The denominations, with number of boards and agencies responding in parentheses, are:

United Methodist Church (15), United Church of Christ (10), Christian Church (Disciples of Christ) (8), Presbyterian Church in the U.S. (5), United Presbyterian Church in the U.S.A. (5), American Baptist Convention (4), Lutheran Church in America (3), Seventh Day Baptists (3). One agency responded from each of the following: African Methodist Episcopal Church; Armenian Church, Diocese of America; Church of the Brethren; The Episcopal Church; Friends United Meeting; Moravian Church in America; Orthodox Bishops in the Americas; Progressive National Baptist Convention; and Reformed Church in America. In two cases, the denomination was not identified on the returned questionnaire. There was one response from the National Council of Churches.

Tabulation of the questionnaire responses indicated that three-fourths of the agencies claimed that women received the same salaries as men for the same position. None reported that women received more salary and eight agencies reported less salary for the same positions. Eight agencies did not reply. A study of the responses as shown in the table below would indicate either that women were not holding the same types of positions as men or that the respondents were unaware or uncommunicative about the salary differences between men and women professionals.

Three-fifths of the agencies reported that the proportion of employed women had remained about the same for the past ten years. Of the remaining two-fifths, twice as many agencies reported an increase in the proportion of employed women as reported a decrease.

Over the next ten years, three-fourths of the agencies expect the proportion of men and women employed to remain about the same, while the rest of the agencies expect increases. None anticipate decreases.

Women were not excluded by definition from executive positions by four out of five of the agencies. Only ten respondents to the questionnaire indicated such exclusion. Exclusion seemed to be based on the fact that a position called for an ordained person, and women were excluded from ordination. Many positions required theological education which, it was stated, few women have. Some responses seemed to suggest that women employees have their own responsibilities in national boards and agencies such as women's boards.

Three-fifths of the agencies reported that women were employed in executive positions where budgets and policies were decided. About a third of the respondents said they did not employ women at this level at all. Actually one or two women were employed in the majority of these agencies, excluding women's organizations.

Only two church groups had programs of recruitment aimed especially at the employment of women in executive positions. One agency stated that many of its professional jobs require graduate work in Christian Education plus experience as a Director of Religious Education in local churches and that most of those having this type of background were women.

Six agencies reported unusual difficulties in the recruitment and employment of women in executive positions, while the majority (78.5 per cent) had no such problem. Reasons given by the six agencies reporting difficulties centered around the difficulty in finding qualified women, problems relating to hiring married women who must change residence because of shift in husband's assignment to another location, or because the woman professional's assignment calls for a change in residence.

Only four agencies indicated the existence of policy statements or studies on the employment of women. A useful comment from a denominational board is as follows: "The United Christian Missionary Society does have a statement in its Code of Regulations (Constitution) regarding employment of women executives. 'All Executive offices shall be open alike to men and women, except that the President and Vice President shall be of the opposite sex, and it shall be the purpose and duty of the Board of Trustees to keep the Officers as equally divided between men and women as practicable.' "

More than four out of five respondents felt that the performance of women was equal to that of men. None reported it superior, and one thought it inferior because of the "difficulty in dealing with men." Some

NUMBER AND PERCENTAGE DISTRIBUTION OF EXECUTIVE POSITIONS
HELD BY MEN AND WOMEN AND BY SALARY GRADES IN 65 NATIONAL
RELIGIOUS AGENCIES IN 1969

Salary Grades	Number of Positions Reported					
	Total		Women		Men	
	%	Number	%	Number	%	Number
ALL GRADES	100.1	1,558	100.0	389	100.0	1,169
$22,500 & over	0.8	12	—	—	1.0	12
$20,000–22,500	2.4	37	2.0	8	2.5	29
$17,500–20,000	3.5	54	1.3	5	4.2	49
$15,000–17,500	13.8	215	5.9	23	16.4	192
$12,500–15,000	29.2	455	13.4	52	34.5	403
$10,000–12,500	27.5	429	34.2	133	25.3	296
$7,500–10,000	21.0	327	39.1	152	15.0	175
Under $7,500	1.8	29	4.1	16	1.1	13

comments relating to the equality of performance between men and women follow: "Depends upon the training of either the man or the woman.". . . "Our semiannual evaluation of all employees reveals no discernible sex differential in performance of editorial and executive duties.". . . "I have observed no difference in quality [of performance of work assignments] based on sex.". . . "The one level of real difference is that women must (or feel they must) constantly prove themselves as capable or more capable than male peers."

About one-half of the denominational agencies responding to the questionnaire were uncertain (41.5 per cent) or did not report (12.3 per cent) on programs of training and upgrading of skills for professional women on an ecumenical basis. About one-fourth thought this would be helpful, while another one-fourth felt it would not.

The 65 denominational boards and agencies reported on 1,558 positions in total, and 25 per cent were held by women.

Salary grades varied considerably from agency to agency. These were adjusted to fit roughly into the eight grades shown in the table below by use of a standard mathematical procedure. While this might produce some distortion for individual agencies, it provides a reasonable basis for comparative purposes.

For the total number of positions reported, 3.2 per cent were in the $20,000-and-over category as compared with 22.8 per cent in the $10,000-and-under range. For men, 3.5 per cent received $20,000 or more; for women only 2.0 per cent. At the other extreme, 16.1 per cent of the men received under $10,000 as compared with 43.2 per cent of the women. The proportion of men to women is much higher for all salary grades above $12,500. The reverse is the case for all grades below $12,500. The modal grade for men (34.5 per cent) is from $12,500 to $15,000; while for women the modal grade (39.1 per cent) is two steps down ($7,500 to $10,000).

In summary, these data reflect adherence to the rhetoric of equality of opportunity for women and men on the one hand, and the factual conditions of considerable discrimination on the other.

I. Sex Role Stereotyping

While some women's groups stress the issues of discrimination in church employment, hiring practices, ordination, etc., others have begun to call into question the deeper values of the church as expressed through Christian Education materials. Women may become more visible in the structures of the church, but research and close examination of these questions will be crucial in the attempt to free the church from prejudice and stereotyping of women.

The following report on sex role streotyping in the United Methodist nursery curriculum was prepared for the New York Conference Task Force on the Status of Women in the Church by Tilda Norberg and Miriam Crist. This report is preliminary and forms the basis for an expanded study which will be completed by the end of 1970.

SEX ROLE STEREOTYPING IN THE
UNITED METHODIST NURSERY CURRICULUM *

A study was made of curriculum materials for three-year-olds published by the United Methodist Church to discover what was being taught by the curriculum about sex roles. The method was a simple one. Each story, song or picture was examined for evidence of attitudinal bias in the following areas:

1. sex-typing of play activities, behavior and feelings of boys and girls
2. the role of mother and father
3. evidence of girls helping mothers and boys helping fathers
4. occupational sex-typing of men and women.

The study revealed blatant sexual stereotyping of behavior, emotions, abilities, occupations and life style on almost every page. Men and boys were generally shown as active, brave, useful, shaping their environment, and happy in their world. Women and girls were portrayed as passive, powerless, waiting, needing help, watching the action, and often unhappy. In addition, the traditional roles of mother and father were reinforced almost without exception, men and woman were stereotyped occupationally, and it was clear that little girls are expected to follow in their mothers' traditional footsteps.

* Copyright © 1970 by Miriam Crist and Tilda Norberg.

	Attitude	*Number of Occurrences*
SEX-TYPING OF PLAY ACTIVITIES, BEHAVIOR AND FEELINGS OF BOYS AND GIRLS	a. Girls appearing as those who are passive, powerless, waiting on others, needing help and protection, watching the action, unhappy	28
	b. Girls as active in play activities	5
	c. Boys appearing as active, brave, protectors of women, angry, playing with blocks, trucks, etc, in control	31
	d. boys reading or in some other passive activity	3
ROLE OF MOTHER AND FATHER	a. the role of the mother as one who is always around the house, who comforts the child, who does the cleaning, washing, baking, cooking and shopping	24
	b. mother as worker	1
	c. the role of the father as one who is away at work all day, who is home only at night, who travels, who fixes things and who protects the family	22
	d. father doing housework or at home during the day	0
GIRLS HELPING MOTHERS; BOYS HELPING FATHERS	a. evidence of girls helping mothers work	18
	b. evidence of girls helping fathers work	0
	c. evidence of boys helping fathers work	5
	d. evidence of boys helping mothers work	2
OCCUPATIONAL STEREOTYPING OF MEN AND WOMEN	a. the occupations of women as secretaries, office workers, teachers, nurses, organist	9
	b. the occupation of men as doctors, mailmen, firemen, truck drivers, storekeepers	11
	c. the minister as a man	10
	d. the minister as a woman	0
	e. the church schoolteacher as a man	3
	f. the church schoolteacher as a woman	15

1. Sex-Typing of Play Activities, Behavior and Feelings

The way this sex-typing is done can best be illustrated by the curriculum itself:

"Betsy was not ready to go into nursery class. She didn't want to play in her new room. She sat on a chair just inside the door. She watched the boys pile the blocks up. They were noisy. Two girls were setting the table. That looked like fun."

Finally the teacher gently persuades Betsy to play with a doll. The accompanying picture shows a teary-eyed three-year-old girl sitting timidly just inside her classroom. On the next page is a story about Peter, who is shown with two friends happily rolling a ball on the floor. Notice how very much more self-sufficient Peter is than Betsy.

"When Peter came to nursery class he wanted to play. He tried a puzzle. He did it all by himself. He looked at a book all by himself. He pushed a train across the floor all by himself . . . All the children came to Peter. All the children wanted to play roll the ball with Peter. All the children were Peter's friends."

Other stories carry on in the same vein.

"Marcia didn't feel right inside, not sick—just a little unhappy. Mrs. Johns noticed and knew. Mrs. Johns took Marcia's hand. She wanted to help. 'Sometimes you feel alone, all by yourself,' Mrs. Johns said. Marcia came closer. She felt better being closer to Mrs. Johns. The teacher knew, she cared, she wanted to help."

Again in this story, the girl is shown as unhappy and needing help. She is a victim of her own emotions, dependent on others. Instead of asking for what she needs, she waits for the teacher to notice. Of course, all three-year-old children need help, and need it often, but the point is that this curriculum portrays only girls in this way. In fact, girls were *usually* shown as needing help, while boys were *usually* shown as self-sufficient. In one notable story entitled *Helping Jimmy*, a boy is helped by his classmates, but the twist of the story is that he has had an accident and his leg is in a cast. . . .

In a story about a turtle, Wendy squeals when the turtle touches her leg and she is afraid to pick it up, but Brad and Tom fearlessly handle the animal and make a little pen for it out of blocks.

"Clink, clink. Brad put his money in the basket on the beauty center. The teacher helped Wendy open her purse so she could get her money out."

"The farmer gave the children a special treat. He let each one of them pick a pumpkin, any one they liked. Brian pulled his from the vine all by himself. Missy needed the teacher to help with hers."

In the Summer 1967 curriculum, there are two "hero" tales about boys who averted disaster by their quick thinking; one reported a fire, the other rescued a girl who was too small to cross the street alone. There are no comparable stories of girls in any of the materials examined.

In a story entitled "Mary Ann's Special Day," the heroine waits in tense anxiety (holding her brother's hand) during her class for someone to remember to sing "Happy Birthday" to her. There were no "waiting" stories about boys; however, girls were frequently shown in this way. Even in the nursery, girls are being taught to wait until someone gives them attention, rather than going after what they want. Later they will be taught to wait for boy friends, for dates, for marriage proposals, for husbands to come home from work, etc. A person who is waiting for something to happen to her is dependent on the actions of the others, thus she is a victim rather than a shaper of her environment.

In another story, a boy offers to take care of his mother.

Throughout the curriculum, girls play with dolls and dishes, while boys play with trucks, wagons, balls, and puzzles.

Of course, there is nothing wrong or harmful about any one of these stories individually. But because the attitudes documented above are presented consistently, and almost exclusively, a very powerful and malevolent message comes through. Girls are *taught* by this (and other) reinforcement to be helpless, frightened, passive, waiting and weak. Boys are taught to be active, protective of females, capable and strong. This setting up of expectations based on sex has nothing to do with characteristics of individual children, and thus it places a strain on both boys and girls. But, by any standard, girls are more handicapped by this curriculum than boys, for the characteristics attributed to girls are far more debilitating, restrictive and humiliating than those ascribed to boys.

II. Role of Mother and Father

With only one exception, mothers were portrayed in their traditional role of homemaker, child-rearer, and volunteer worker. The exception was a single instance of a working mother—referred to indirectly in a story about mother and father taking a child to a day-care center. In only two instances were there baby-sitters in the home, and in one of those situations it was clearly stated that mother was away only when attending meeting. This, inspite of the fact that 29 million women in America work, many as the sole family breadwinner.

Fathers were portrayed as the breadwinners, the ones who work, travel, fix things, and protect their families.

In two stories about what mothers and fathers do, it is stated that father cares for his family and his house. He goes to work, but always comes back at night. Mother is near whenever the child needs her. She helps hurt places, she keeps the home clean and loves the children. The implication is that parental love is expressed in the traditional role system, and that other family life styles are aberrations, and not consistent with the way things are supposed to be.

Thus, children learn that if their mother works, they are somehow being cheated, rather than enriched, as they are by father's work. A girl learns that her "true destiny" is to be a wife and mother (who does not work), and boys are taught that while they must do something to earn money as an adult, a very wide range of possibilities is open to them.

III. Girls Helping Mothers; Boys Helping Fathers

As might be expected, girls in this curriculum help their mothers much more than boys help their mothers or their fathers. In fact, girls are shown helping in the home more than twice as many times as boys. In no instance did girls help their fathers with work. Thus, by age three or four, expectations for a girl's future are already set; she is to flow naturally from helping mother at home to running a home of her own. A boy's future is much more open, but less continuous with his childhood. Although he helps at home, he is much less home-oriented right from the beginning. His parents cannot know what he will need to learn for his future work, for he could become anything from a store clerk to a doctor.

IV. Occupational Sex-Typing of Men and Women

The identification of men's and women's occupations is thoroughly traditional in the curriculum. Thus, women are shown as helpers of men, e.g. nurses or secretaries. Moreover, the women workers were never equated with mothers, although some of the men whose occupations were talked about were identified as fathers. Thus a job and motherhood were shown to be mutually exclusive. All of the ministers shown were males. What of the potential female ministers enrolled in nursery class? Most of the church school teachers shown were women. What of the little boys who someday might enjoy teaching church school? (One of the male teachers shown was only substituting for his wife.)

Conclusion

We believe it has been demonstrated that the United Methodist nursery curriculum is immersed in the sex-role caste system and, therefore, is particularly limiting for girls, which is then contrary to good principles of education and to the Gospel.

Two things must be done. A much more elaborate study must be undertaken of the Methodist curriculum for all age groups, including adults. Then, the curriculum must be revised toward a more equitable sharing between the sexes of characteristics discussed in this report . . . which are *human*, not *sexual*.

J.   Women and the Priesthood

*A concern for the situation of women in the church has led to re-
newed interest in the role of the minister's wife. The conflicting demands
imposed on her are seen as an extreme example of the role stereotyping
of women within the church and the general culture as well. Unlike
other areas of concern, however, a fair amount of research has been
done on the role conflicts of women who marry ministers and on the
effect of these conflicts on the man's ministry.*

*This article on women and the priesthood was originally published
by PMV—Pro Mundi Vita, International Center for Information and
Documentation, Brussels and summarizes the results of studies of pastors' wives in America, Holland, France and the Near East.*

One of the major transformations of our society concerns the status
of the woman. This status has evolved markedly, effecting in its own
evolution other social changes in many fields.

Many of these changes are already affecting and will increasingly
affect the church as human society.

In this short note we cannot of course attempt to compile a complete
inventory of the repercussions of the transformations in the status of the
woman on the church. We should like merely to draw the attention of
the decision-makers in the church to some of the problems which are
now arising through the relations between the priesthood and the female
world.

Our purpose however is not doctrinal, but sociological. We do not
intend to enter the debate on the compatibilities between the priesthood
and the female sex, *i.e.*, can women exercise the priestly ministry or not?
It is known that this matter is under debate. It is certainly a sign of the
times. It is known that it can, if it is settled in the affirmative, profoundly shake the foundations of a church, as has been demonstrated
by recent experience in the Swedish church. It is also known that in
Germany for example, at the core of the evangelical church, over five
hundred women are today exercising the pastoral ministry.

Leaving aside this precise question, we should like to clear up the
question of the relations between the woman and the man in charge of
a pastoral ministry when they are bound together by marriage. In the
Eastern Catholic church, in the Orthodox church, in many Protestant
churches and, from now on, in the order of the diaconate within the
Latin church, many women are the wives of men engaged in the ministry. What is this married situation like? What kind of women agree to

share their lot with a pastor of souls? What problems must these women resolve? What difficulties must they surmount?

Of course we should like to be able to answer in a precise way to these questions. However, we are obliged to limit ourselves to the information available. Not making this a doctrinal task, but a sociological one, we are restricted to advancing nothing which has not formed the object of precise observation and in general of a serious enquiry. But unfortunately there is very little positive research in this field. To our knowledge, there only exist the following works:

1. Wallace Denton, *The Role of the Minister's Wife,* Philadelphia, Westminster, 1962, and *The Minister's Wife as a Counselor,* Philadelphia, Westminster, 1965.
2. William Douglas, *Ministers' Wives,* New York, Harper & Row, 1965.
3. Robert Clément, "La vie du clergé marié en Orient," in *Proche Orient Chrétien,* 16, 1966, 354–378, English translation: "The Life of the Married Eastern Clergy," in *Eastern Churches Review,* 1, 1968, 387–394.
4. Christine Smalbrugge-Hack, "Verslag van het onderzoek dat gehouden werd door de Bond van Nederlandse Predikanten, onder vrouwen van predikanten voor gewone werkzaamheden," in *Het orgaan van de Bond van Nederlandse Predikanten,* July-August 1966.
5. Francine Dumas, "Enquête et réflexions sur la femme de pasteur et le ministère pastoral," in *Etudes Théologiques et Religieuses,* 38, 1963, 3, 9–19.

There exist some American studies earlier than those listed here, but they do not contribute any elements which are not reproduced better by the study of W. Douglas. There is a study bearing on the family situation of 370 Protestant pastors who have abandoned the ministry in the work by G. J. Jud, E. W. Mills, G. W. Burch, *Ex-Pastors: Why Men Leave the Parish Ministry,* Philadelphia, Pilgrim, 1969. In Great Britain a still unpublished inquiry was undertaken by the Department of Social Studies of the University of Newcastle upon Tyne, under the leadership of the Rev. Dr W. Pickering on *The Place of Married Students and their Wives in British Theological Colleges.* An ecumenical cross-section of 300 married students and their wives were interviewed on the system of theological formation and its effects on married life.

We propose to divide the results of the researches in question into four geographical areas, describing the American, French, Dutch and Eastern situations.

1. The American situation

The studies we have available for the United States are certainly the most satisfying yet, in that they cover an immense field of observation.

One can in fact estimate the number of American pastors at around 220,000. The majority being married, the number of pastors' wives is, as can be seen, considerable. The most detailed and extensive study is that by Douglas. It is this study we shall now discuss. The author was engaged in the study of the main American Protestant denominations: Baptists, Methodists, Episcopalians, Lutherans, Presbyterians, Disciples of Christ, etc., to which about half the body of pastors belong. A representative sample of these some 100,000 pastors was constituted and a 12-page questionnaire sent to the wives. Once the replies were obtained, 4,777 of them could be utilized with a view to results. On the basis of these replies, Douglas proposes the following typology:

a. Pastors' wives in the proportion of 20.6 per cent describe themselves as collaborators of their husband in the pastoral work which they both consider as teamwork. They share its responsibilities, assume complementary roles and feel equally engaged in the apostolate. The woman considers herself, equally with her husband, separated from the ordinary faithful by the irreducible originality of the pastoral mission. The presence of children is an undeniable extra burden accepted in itself, but also in a spirit of sacrifice and with a view to giving a good example.

b. A larger group, representing 63.9 per cent of the pastors' wives, consider themselves involved in pastoral work in quite a different sense: these women consider it their task to assist their husband, not in first place by sharing his activities, but in the background, sharing his cares. They consider themselves as ordinary Christians having the same responsibilities as the other members of the community and obliged to be good wives and good mothers. They do not wish to play any role of leadership or inspiration in the community, although they will accept occasional participation just like other women. The assistance they bring to their husband is mainly that of a happy, encouraging, believing home. Their children occupy much of their time, in a well-run household where they consider it important to be perfect hostesses in spite of the unpredictable timetables of the husband and the faithful.

c. The other pastors' wives, representing 15.1 per cent (the remaining 0.4 per cent being unclassifiable under the three types mentioned) consider themselves not involved in the ministry of their husband, with two important nuances:

1. One group are satisfied with the role their husband plays but do not feel more involved in the affairs of the church than any other women and not even more than if their husband exercised another profession; they feel in any case very free, very detached, in relation to the role played by their husband, while they will sometimes accept the constraints inherent in it only with an effort;

2. The others bear relatively badly the constraints imposed by the pastoral duties of the husband; they feel frustrated and confined in a role which they find burdensome; they regard the community as an obstacle to the more intimate contact they wish to have with their husband (in all, this type represents scarcely 4 per cent of the total).

The description of these three types, based on the level of involvement in pastoral duties and the degree of satisfaction, leaves out any differences which might be marked from many other points of view (social class, family climate, income, type of work of the husband and possibly of the wife, number of children, standard of education, ministerial rank of the husband, age, region, denomination, size of the community, etc.).

One can however conclude that in the majority of cases the households of the pastors are a success. (In a study entitled "Career Change in the Protestant Ministry," published in *Ministry Studies*, 3, 1969, 5–21, E. W. Mills notes the replies of sixty pastors who explain why they have abandoned their work. Four of them state as dominant motive acute marital difficulties.) They are not substantially affected by the particular difficulties they face, among which the following must be singled out:

a. The wives of pastors have problems quite analogous to wives of executives. They live in spite of all in the shadow of their husband, who is often absent, and these women do not even have, for people from outside, a very marked personality. They are the wives of someone more important than themselves.

b. Pastors' wives do not have the satisfaction of the wives of executives (or of doctors . . .) who can tell themselves that if their husband works more—and is thus more often away from her and the children— he earns more. In fact, if their husband works more he does not generally earn more, but is more often away from her.

c. The wives of pastors must generally be content with modest incomes which do not allow them to compare themselves from this point of view with other women of their condition and which hinder them from having access, as they would often wish, to the cultural possibilities of the society in which they live.

d. The wives of pastors must confront, often several times in their life, the problem of the relations with the community of which the husband is in charge. These relations depend naturally on the way in which the wife conceives her part, but also on the way in which the community conceives the role of the pastor's wife. These do not always coincide. In any case the pastor's wife feels obliged to give constantly a good example and, for some, this obligation is a burden.

The final recommendation of the American study bears on the necessity of not reducing the wives of pastors to a stereotype, which would not allow them to develop their non-interchangeable personality. The wives of pastors wish to be recognized as persons and not be automatically classed, not bound to tasks they would not freely take on, even though the majority are disposed to accept in the faith the responsibilities inherent in the profession of their husband. This recommendation is addressed to the ecclesiastical authorities just as much as to the husbands and the communities, whose demands should be generally better defined and more adapted to the individual.

II. The Dutch situation

If the American situation appears relatively well documented, the Dutch situation is much less so through lack of works of analogous breadth. Nevertheless we do have available the results of the research of the Sociological Institute of the Reformed Church (*Hervormde* [Reformed] Kerk is not to be confused with the *Gereformeerde* Kerk). Under the auspices of the league of Dutch pastors (Bond van Nederlandse Predikanten) 1566 questionnaires were sent to the wives of pastors, of which 762 were returned with a reply. The representativity of these 762 replies is not assured and the author who published the results of the inquiry did not conceal this. In spite of this limitation, the results obtained are nevertheless still preferable to subjective impressions.

It is interesting to point out that 85.6 per cent of those who replied come from practising families, that they rarely had university education (8 per cent), that the majority (80.3 per cent) exercised a profession before their marriage, especially in education (26.1 per cent).

The majority of the pastors' wives (77.5 per cent) exercise a leading role in one or more activities of pastoral type (Sunday school, clubs for young girls, women's associations, aid to old people, etc.); 69 per cent even play a leading role in more than one group; generally these groups are for women or young girls.

The majority of the pastors' wives (77.3 per cent) consider it is up to them to pay visits to old people, to the sick and to women during confinement in their community. Half also receive visits at home (more than five persons per week).

Few pastors' wives (14.8 per cent) on the other hand do any administrative work in the service of their husband or their community. Some (12.2 per cent) work outside the framework of their community, either occasionally (4.1 per cent) or regularly (8.1 per cent), but often part time and generally in education.

When one questions the wives of pastors on the difficulties they encounter, they generally cite the difficulties which are not necessarily peculiar to the profession of their husband, such as absence of the husband during the evening, lack of household help or the necessity of living in a glasshouse. Just under half (45 per cent) cite more specific difficulties:

—the continual efforts demanded by the expectations of the community (regular practice of all religious ceremonies, running women's associations, visits to be paid or received, etc.);

—even when one can respond without too much difficulty to the expectations of the community, the tension remains, provoked by the wish to keep a balance between family life and the expectations of the community;

—the frequent absence of the husband and father, particularly during the weekend;

—the generally modest salary of the husband, and the obligation to keep up quite a big house, which is not chosen by the couple themselves and which they must always be prepared to leave;

—the exceptional situation of the pastor's wife, which is one of solitude in the midst of multiple relations.

Faced with these difficulties, what is the degree of satisfaction of the pastors' wives? How do they face up to them?

—bear them badly, find them too great and would like a different life	5.9%
—find them a great burden	12.7%
—find them bearable	72.3%
—find them easy to bear	9.3%

Could some concrete improvements be brought to their kind of life? The question was asked and the replies were oriented often towards household help or a raise in salary. Some suggested better pastoral formation (58.7 per cent would like conferences for pastors' wives to be organized regularly). Several would like the work hours of their husbands to be better fixed, so that they could take a holiday, particularly after especially heavy periods, and have some Sundays off.

The conclusions of the author who presents the results of the inquiry, Christine Smalbrugge-Hack, could be summarized as follows:

1. The great majority of the wives of pastors are happy to play the role they do in their community;

2. They feel they need continued formation. They cannot be satisfied with the catechism of their youth.

3. They should be the object of a particular pastoral task on the part of the church.

4. They should have arranged for them free Sundays and holidays.

5. The pastor's pay is often low and the attention of the church must be kept alert on this matter.

6. The communities must take up a position in relation to the pastor's family as being responsible for them, being prompted by present necessities and not outdated traditions.

In a collective work entitled *Over de predikant,* Utrecht, Ambo, 1969, the author of this enquiry published a contribution, "De predikantsvrouw" pp. 116–132, which continues her ideas on the subject. She affirms that if the pastors were celibate the church would lose by this fact alone a great number of its most faithful collaborators (i.e. the pastors' wives). Wondering about future perspectives, she believes that the pastor's wife will have less and less a separate function in the church but, as all the other members of the community, will have to bear the responsibility for her gifts and talents both in the church and in society.

III. The French situation

The French inquiry we have available is presented by Francine Dumas, the wife of pastor André Dumas, professor of ethics at the Faculty of Theology of Paris. It is a regional inquiry. We do not know what region was chosen, nor how many wives replied to the inquiry. The results seem even less assuredly representative than those of the Dutch inquiry but, once again, they are preferable to subjective appraisals.

The first part of the inquiry sought to define what were in fact the activities of the pastors' wives. In 80 per cent of cases the wives cited visits, mainly paid and sometimes received; in 70 per cent of cases the participation in women's groups, then choirs and Sunday schools. The majority, moreover, cite a broad selection of tasks which can become really wearisome. They would generally like to go to fewer meetings, especially fewer church meetings, in order to be able to enter into contact with the outside world and devote more time to visits. Some showed a desire for a better theological and biblical formation.

A second series of questions concerned the life of the couple. The very varied replies do not allow one to form a general outline of the role of the wife in a pastor's household. The question remains open on a situation of fact: the church does not officially associate the wife in the ministry of her husband, does not acknowledge to her any precise responsibility, but counts on her availability. In so doing, acknowledges Francine Dumas, the church "decides in fact on the fate of a being it does not employ and whose ministry it does not recognize."

Today, roughly two choices are open to pastors' wives:

a. They can be simply the wife of the pastor. In this case, she is not bound to the contract which binds the pastor to his parish, she is a laywoman like the others in charge of her children and could possibly, if she has few children or if they are old enough, take on a job—a decision which would concern the couple and not the church. She would have to assist the pastor to fulfill his role well, not by associating herself with it but by making him happy and available for the service of the church.

b. The other choice envisages the woman sharing the pastoral responsibilities as completely as possible. One would then have to do with a real pastoral couple. The parish then has at its service a man and a woman who bear with it the tasks of the church, which vary according to the great diversity of needs and of individuals.

The inquiry in question does not tell us the proportion of women who choose such and such a concept of their role. We have asked pastors with a wide knowledge to estimate this proportion. According to them, the majority would have made the second choice, i.e., what we have called the pastoral couple. This proportion, it can be seen, is notably higher than in the United States where it was preferred by only about one wife in five (but in France it is a matter of estimates and in the United States of replies by quite a representative cross-section).

The difficulties inherent in the role of the pastor's wife are brought out very little in the French inquiry. But the difficulty is discussed of bringing up children when the father is often absent, resources are slender, pastoral secrets often pose questions to one and the other, etc.

In general, however, it is estimated that the households of pastors are usually a success. "The spiritual quality of the majority of pastors is generally enriched by their wife" notes one of our correspondents.

A movement is emerging in France that the inquiry of Francine Dumas merely touches on in passing (the latter dates from 1963) but which seems to be becoming definite. It appears "that the wives of pastors are taking more and more an independent occupation, paid or unpaid. This is not primarily to augment the budget or to follow a fashion of emancipation, but because the woman, like the man, needs to realize herself or, more simply, to let her acquired degree of culture bear fruit, after the period of births and infancy of the children." Which another pastor echoes while acknowledging that "the young pastors who claim to exercise a profane profession on top of their ministry do not take into account that the ministry is also a profession," which is a way of pointing out an evolution of the concept entertained of the ministry both by the men and the women attached to the pastoral service of the church.

IV. The Eastern situation

The facts we have available for the Catholic Church of Eastern rite are not comparable to the foregoing. The inquiry was carried out not among the wives of the priests but among the married priests themselves. It dates from Winter 1965 and received 97 replies, coming mainly from Lebanon, Syria, Jordan and Iraq. As it can be estimated that a third of the priests from these countries are married, the replies received cannot claim to be a representative cross-section.

As they are furthermore very inexplicit on the feminine problems proper, even as viewed by men, and as the married clergy is not today, notably owing to the policy of the Congregation for the Eastern Church, "of a very high intellectual worth, nor very educated spiritually," no conclusions can be drawn from this inquiry from the point of view we are concerned with here.

Father Clement acknowledges that "in view of the weak intellectual standard of this clergy, it is difficult today for a seminarian to find an educated fiancée"; consequently their wives come from lower class backgrounds, which does not hinder them at all from giving "as a rule the example of Christian and sound family life" to their many children.

Many priests acknowledge that marriage balances their priestly life and even that "their priesthood gains by coexisting with marriage." From the facts reproduced by the presenter of the inquiry one sees emerging, it seems, a strong majority of women bringing an indirect aid to their husband by being good mothers and good wives. More rare seem those who will say, like one priest, "the missionary activity of my wife is incontestably of great assistance for my ministry"; more easily they will emphasize that "the wife of the parish priest helps him very much to understand his parishioners, especially the women." One can also point out the preference in the villages for married priests; people do not seem to have absolute confidence in the virtue of celibate priests. The material difficulties of the married clergy are, alas, sometimes, if not always, chronic.

Father Clement ends his study with a plea for the re-evaluation of the married clergy.

Need we conclude?

The preceding pages being already the summary of conclusions drawn from several thousand replies, it is not at all worthwhile to attempt a simplifying supersynthesis.

What is obvious in any case is the wish of the pastors' wives to be treated as individuals and not as stereotyped entities. This wish to be individuals, more pronounced without doubt today, does not allow for a reduction of the problems of the pastoral couple to a few diagrammatic features. Two trends seem, however, to be emerging—one which would make of the pastor's wife a real collaborator in the pastoral ministry, another which would give her a role of indirect aid as wife and mother. It would seem that the first trend predominates in Europe and the second in the United States, where the great majority of wives are satisfied to be the wife of a man of the church.

The very general impression is that the marriage of the pastors is a success and that the ministry, as also the marriage, are reciprocally enriched by the sharing of married life.

(Translated from the French)

January 1970

**K.   Report of the National Conference on the
        Role of Women in Theological Education**

*The issues of women's liberation in the church have perhaps come
most alive among women in the seminaries. In many areas where there
is more than one school, the women have begun to relate to one another, to meet and discuss common problems, and in some instances to
form organized groups to bring specific issues to the attention of the
administration and faculty of their respective schools. The joint efforts
of seminary women in the Boston area has resulted in these proposals
regarding women's studies at the Boston Theological Institute and research programs on women in theological education and the church
which are among the most comprehensive statements by women of
their perception of the church and of the necessity for institutional response to the needs and demands of women. These proposals constitute
the report of the National Conference on the Role of Women in Theological Education which was held May 15–17, 1970.*

CONSULTANTS PARTICIPATING IN THE CONFERENCE WEEKEND

Rev. Peggy Way—University of
    Chicago Divinity School
Nelle Morton—Drew Seminary
Dr. Mary Daly—Boston College
Dr. Elizabeth Farians—Loyola
    University
Arlene Swidler—*Journal of Ecu-
    menical Studies*

Dr. Pauli Murray—Lawyer and
    faculty member at Brandeis
Dr. Marlene Dixon—McGill
    University
Sister Marie Augusta Neal—
    Emmanuel College

STUDENTS PARTICIPATING IN THE CONFERENCE WEEKEND

Susan Nevius—Boston Univer-
    sity School of Theology
Sister Mary Bride—Episcopal
    Theological School
Rev. Emily Preston—Andover
    Newton Theological School
Rev. Patricia Doyle—Harvard
    Divinity School
Betty B. White—Episcopal Theo-
    logical School
Sister Janice Raymond—
    Andover Newton Theological
    School

Sue Hyatt—alumna of Episcopal
    Theological School
Pam Marino—Andover Newton
    Theological School
Carol Robb—Boston University
    School of Theology
Linda Capuano—Andover New-
    ton Theological School
Dee Crabtree—Andover New-
    ton Theological School

RATIONALE FOR THE PROPOSED INSTITUTE ON WOMEN

In attempting to outline a rationale for a research center and Institute on Women to be initiated within the Boston Theological Institute in the near future, certain presuppositions must be considered. Indeed, one of the aims of the Institute itself is to examine its own presuppositions for which, given the present state of research concerning the subject, we now have only some clues.

As the whole women's liberation movement has tried to emphasize, the women's revolution is not just another revolution among others, but rather strikes at the heart of the other forms of revolution (race, poverty, war). There are many forms of oppression but, as Simone de Beauvoir has suggested, sex oppression may well be the oldest, most primordial and the most universal form.

This rationale is not a dogmatic statement, but rather it sets forth certain hypotheses to be explored in the research of the Institute. There are, however, certain clues in our society which suggest that there is an integral connection between sexual alienation and the wider forms of social alienation. These clues suggest that the oppression of women as the most universal form of exploitation supports and perpetuates the other forms of exploitation. One needs only to think of the militaristic Pentagon general, the hyper-competitive male in the office, and the pompous, intransigent church official.

The way women are seen in society is a prime determinant in the whole social system. We refuse to consider our movement as one among others. We question that it should be lined up side by side with studies on poverty, racism, etc., because our hypothesis is that it undergirds these other movements.

One of the unique aspects of the women's movement is that it hits directly at interpersonal relationships. This is a particular problem because men and women are so enmeshed in intimate relationship to each other. Therefore it cannot be considered simply in terms of class against class.

We have deliberately chosen the church as locus for the Institute on Women because we consider the church to be particularly significant. Why is this? First, the church has always been an oppressor of women and indeed one of the most oppressive of institutions. Second, we are committed to authentic religious values. This means that true religion fosters the fullest creative development of the individual and excludes all forms of oppression. We are outraged that the church has betrayed its calling. If the church is to be an agent of revolution and reconciliation, women must be authentically integrated as equals into the fabric of its structures and aid it to go beyond presently existing structures.

Third, although there are many variations within the women's liberation movement, few of these have been directly concerned with the
church.

Now we want to influence the church at its most central part—
through the seminaries, because as female Christians we see the church
as a potential revolutionary force in society, if only it can foster authentic "sexual relationships" and full personhood for women. We are
now confronted with a growing women's liberation movement of such
proportions that it can no longer be ignored. The young women who
are the vanguard of this movement generally have bypassed the church
because they see that the church has negated its revolutionary potential
through what it has been doing to women and that in so doing it has
been distorting its own doctrines about the nature and dignity of women
(as well as doctrines about the Christ, the sacraments, and the nature of
the church itself). What we want to do is release this force of social
revolution which is the church. To do this, women, its largest constituency, must be encouraged to realize their personhood within the
church. Otherwise, as in the case of every other major social revolution,
the church will be bypassed. What we are really seeking is not simply
equality for women but the humanization of the species, men and
women. This can only be brought about if men and women discard the
old stereotyped roles in a more authentic search for personhood. In
order for this to be accomplished, pastoral encouragement will be necessary as well as the backing of church leadership. For this reason the
Boston Theological Institute should be in the forefront of the movement.

RESEARCH DESIGN

One of the primary aims of the program would be research. That is,
the Institute on Women should be not merely educational in the sense
of transference of knowledge but creative in new research which will
open up unexplored areas. Our research center will investigate the hypothesis that the women's movement is a most fundamental and unique
movement. The research center will concentrate in several areas:

Regarding *theology:* We would want to determine how theological concepts have fed into the problem of the oppression of
women. We want to approach this problem on the most radical
theological level. Inevitably it raises the problem of God and God
language. It raises also the problem of Christ. We must ask whether
Christianity, which appears to be inherently male centered, can
be truly instrumental in women's liberation. Moreover, we must

ask whether there is any hope for Mariology—could it be transformed and made supportive of women's liberation instead of deprecating women? The whole system of sacraments and symbols would have to be seen in a different perspective.

Regarding *ethics:* We would want to examine the function of the church in society as supportive of legal systems that oppress women. The liberation of married women, for example, has in some ways been opposed by the church. In view of the sort of insights that come to the fore from reading such books as *The Biological Time Bomb* (Taylor), for example, one becomes aware of ethical issues that will arise in the future, such as problems in genetics. We are coming to realize that the church's thinking in such matters is outmoded. Moreover, such present pressing problems as abortion, divorce, birth control, and unwed motherhood have to be dealt with from a pastoral and an ethical perspective.

Regarding the *sociology of religion:* This research will be both theoretical and statistical. We will want to see variations within the movement at present, the breakdown into categories of its constituency, and how it relates to the larger social system. We might want also to explore de Beauvoir's thesis that capitalism is the greatest obstruction to feminism. The democratization of the church goes hand in hand with women's liberation. We can no longer think of the church in hierarchical patterns, since the most ancient hierarchy is the man-woman hierarchy. Wouldn't it naturally follow from women's liberation that there would be democratization of the church? As far as Roman Catholics and Episcopalians are concerned, we might think of religious orders. The problem is that these have traditionally been supportive of the feminine mystique although ambiguously. In view of recent movements such as the formation of the National Coalition of American Nuns, is it possible that the sisterhoods which were formerly supportive of the feminine mystique could become instruments of women's liberation within the church?

Regarding *Church History:* The history of the church's discrimination against women will have to be explored. Moreover there are special problems. For example, the church and Marxist society have traditionally appeared to be enemies, yet there is a relationship between women's liberation and Marxism. Possibly by liberating women in general, Marxism is then contributing to the liberation of women within the church itself. The implications of this should also be explored in connection with the Christian–Marxist dialogue. Here is a point where Marxism can teach the church something about women's dignity, although ironically, the church has always preached the dignity of women.

Aside from these specialized fields of research, we also propose that some of the work of the center be interdisciplinary. Interdisciplinary studies should be made in relation to law, biology, political science, sociology, anthropology, psychology, etc. We must think also in terms of dialogue with futurists and generalists, anticipating problems that will arise in the future.

It is most appropriate that Boston has been chosen as the center for the Institute on Women. We have seven theological schools which are members of the Boston Theological Institute. Moreover, the director, Dr. Walter Wagoner, has expressed willingness to help and support such a program. Furthermore, in addition to the theological schools, there are at hand great centers of scientific research such as Massachusetts Institute of Technology. In addition to the geographical factor, it is evident that the time factor favors the establishment of such a program now. We note the current explosion of the question in the mass media. Even the grass-roots level of consciousness is being affected. It is in fact a time of consciousness raising on the part of men and women. The Boston Theological Institute should take responsibility *now* for the analysis and promotion of this consciousness-raising process on the level of serious research.

CURRICULUM

We envision the program as being a joint project wherein faculty and students together are engaged in a creative enterprise of research and learning which is mutual. For this reason, it is important not to make a sharp distinction between research and curriculum since courses will feed into research and research into curriculum. With this in mind we propose the following general course outline.

Theology. There should be a creative course which attempts radically to rethink traditional concepts (for example, of God, Christ, the church, the sacraments) in the perspective of women't liberation. The underlying premise would be that the traditional conceptualizations are demeaning to women and that a radical reorientation will be necessary. It will be important therefore to ask such questions as whether God should be called "he," whether masculine images of God can suffice, whether there is value in trying to use mother images as well as father images of God, whether it is more desirable to transcend all anthropomorphic imagery, whether Christology must be reconceptualized in view of the liberation of women, whether Mariology works against women's liberation necessarily or whether it can offer insights in favor of women's liberation, whether ecclesiology should be reconceptualized (for example, it is problematic that the church is symbolized as the bride of Christ and yet is dominated by a male hierarchy).

Ethics. An unbiased approach is needed for problems related to sex. Moreover, it will also be necessary to examine the ethics of sexism as expressed in the mass media, literature, and the arts. The course should also investigate sexism as it is expressed in job and educational discrimination, psychological and psychiatric counseling. The ethics of the double standard of morality should be carefully examined. New ethical problems that will present themselves in the future should be examined. For example, there are problems that will arise from genetics, such as determination of sex before birth (Will the bias against females in our society result in overpopulation of males?).

Church History. It would be important to examine the history of the church's antifeminism as reflected in such documents as the Bible, the writings of the Church Fathers, the medieval theologians, the popes, and recent theological writings. It is also important to investigate such matters as the existence of deaconesses in the early church. The history of religious orders of women should be studied with special reference to outstanding leaders such as abbesses (for example, abbesses of double monasteries). The history of canon law and ecclesiastical custom regarding marriage and the cloister should be examined. The course should also look into the lives of outstanding women who were not members of religious orders, such as Eleanor of Aquitaine. It would be important also to study the church's reactions to the early stages of the feminist movement as well as to more recent events such as the divorce controversy in Italy.

Bible. The course should examine such texts as the stories of the creation and of the fall in Genesis. It should study Old Testament history and the history of Jewish law concerning women as expressed in the Biblical texts. New Testament study should examine the outstandingly antifeminine Pauline tests. The emphasis throughout should be upon the historic and social context of the documents in question.

Sociology of Religion. It is essential that the course in sociology of religion be given a position of central importance and that the course reflect and feed into a high level of research such as detailed in the research design above.

Church and Law. The course should examine the role of the church in relation to legal systems that have been and still are oppressive to women.

Professional Courses. These should apply the material from the research-oriented courses described above to the practical problems of Christian ministry.

FIELD AND CLINICAL PASTORAL EDUCATION

Field Education

In any consideration of field education, there must be the underlying assumption that field education is an *actual ministry* as well as an opportunity wherein students learn to make decisions and gain professional competence in various areas. Field education is also a situation wherein the student begins to search out what she is or is not going to do after graduation and entrance into the professional ministry.

Policies: Because field education is actual participation in the work of the ministry, it is legitimate and necessary to give credit for any and all such work; because field education is participation in the active ministry, in schools where field education is required the school should provide active support (financial as well as psychological) for students involved in field education.

We believe that field education credit and funding should be given to students who choose to participate in field education programs involving women's liberation group activities in fulfillment of their field work requirement.

Field education should further provide opportunities for women students in Boston Theological Institute to work in ministries which deal with women or specific groups of women such as divorcées, welfare mothers, prostitutes, etc. These ministries should also be involved in exploring issues which affect women.

There should be provision made within the field education programs of the B.T.I. schools to train women students who will train women on the local and national church levels to assume responsible and leadership roles.

Clinical Pastoral Education

More attention needs to be given in clinical pastoral education to the special problems of women in counseling situations. It is absolutely necessary in order to insure that such attention be given to these problems that numbers of female supervisors be added in clinical programs of the various B.T.I. schools.

STUDENT WELFARE

A large portion of the Institute on Women must be concerned with student welfare. This encompasses such areas as recruitment, scholarships, and student life.

At present, little or no effort is made to recruit women into the various B.T.I. schools. Indeed, the two Catholic seminaries of St. John's and Weston do not even admit women to their full-time degree enrollments. We are outraged at this overt discriminatory practice and strongly urge that such schools which refuse to admit women as full-time degree students be deprived of B.T.I. funding and resources. We fail to recognize how this nonadmission policy of the Catholic seminaries can be regarded as anything but discriminatory and insulting not only to Catholic women but to all women interested in theological education and ministry. The ecumenical barriers that such discriminatory practices set up are of the gravest nature. As far as the other B.T.I. schools are concerned, an intensely active program of recruitment is necessary. To do this, we advise that the present B.T.I. recruitment officers of the various schools consult and co-operate with the director of the Institute on Women in a sincere effort to recruit women students.

We also feel strongly that the various B.T.I. schools must further encourage women students by making available financial aid in the form of grants and scholarships. One of the tasks of the director of the Institute on Women would be just this (see section regarding the duties of the director).

In order to keep women students in seminaries and theological schools, however, there are certain problems of student life that will necessitate radical overhauling. Such problems include housing (on some campuses); inept counseling services which fail to encourage women to break out of their static situations; the imposition of denigrating self-images upon women students by their professors and male colleagues; discriminatory practices on the part of professors and administrators; and the problem of male chauvinistic attitudes regarding why women are in seminary.

Included in this area of student life is also the problem of the minister's wife. Overlooked by seminary education in general, it is she who often supports her husband through theological education and then lags behind him intellectually causing later rejection by some husbands. This, of course, is related in general to the problem of the inferior status, intellectual, cultural, and social of the minister's wife. The proposed Institute on Women would offer courses and resources to these women at suitable hours and financial arrangements and also work for the establishment of day-care centers in the near future in order to remedy intellectual disparity between husband and wife. The Institute on Women would also want to provide seminars and counseling services for the minister's wife which would not merely foster her adjustment to traditional roles but would serve to liberate her to reject these roles in favor of self-actualization.

ADMINISTRATION AND BUDGET

Steering Committee

Function. The duties of the steering committee in conjunction with the executive director of Boston Theological Institute will be to first hire a woman director for the Institute on Women. Secondly, the committee, in consultation with the woman director of the Institute, the executive director of Boston Theological Institute, and the Deans of the various B.T.I. schools, will hire faculty and staff personnel (women) to implement the proposed Institute on Women. Thirdly, the steering committee shall be an ongoing decision-making body in conjunction with the B.T.I. executive director and the director of the Institute on Women which makes changes and decisions concerning the proposed Institute on Women.

Composition. The steering committee will be composed of six women and one man. Four of the six women must be women students of the four B.T.I. schools that admit women; one shall be a woman faculty member in the Boston Theological Institute, and the other shall be a woman outside the Boston Theological Institute who is knowledgeable in the area of women's liberation. The male member of the committee must also be informed in the area of women's liberation. These seven members of the steering committee shall be initially chosen by the B.T.I. Women's Conference and will then proceed to elect its own chairwoman and other officers (as it sees fit) from within its own number.

Executive Director of the Institute on Women

The implementation of such a proposed Institute on Women will be impossible without the leadership of a trained, competent and fully committed director. We feel that a certain priority should be given to this most pressing problem. The problem of a director should not be treated as a secondary item. Hiring of the director, as mentioned previously, should be done in conjunction with the steering committee elected by the Women's Conference and with the executive director of

Boston Theological Institute. The duties of the director should include the searching out and the hiring of faculty (hiring being done in conjunction with the steering committee, the executive director of Boston Theological Institute, and the Deans of the respective B.T.I. schools); the handling of problems that may arise regarding the welfare of women students in areas such as recruitment, scholarships, housing, student-professor relationships, counseling, discriminatory attitudes . . . on the part of the men students, ministers' wives, etc.; organization and planning of curriculum in conjunction with the steering committee and the faculty of the Institute on Women; attempting to establish scholarship funds for women through the various B.T.I. schools; the planning of programs and lectureships relative to women's liberation; final decision regarding the distribution of funds for the Institute on Women in matters where it has not already been stipulated that such decisions be made in conjunction with the B.T.I. director and the steering committee; securing further funds for the Institute in conjunction with the B.T.I. director. (It may prove necessary within a short period of time that an administrative assistant to the executive director be hired.)

Field Work Director

It is important that a field work director committed to women's liberation be hired as part of the Institute on Women. Her duties would include the following: She would have to recognize and deal with pastoral problems in relation to preparing women for the ministry. She would have to encourage recognition of the legitimate needs of women for careers. She would have to work out ways and means of overcoming stereotypes and biases as expressed in sermons, hymns, prayers, and counseling. Furthermore, she should work to foster adequate pastoral handling of such matters as birth control, abortion, sex roles, marital relationships, unwed motherhood, adoption, jobs, and careers. She should insure that there be women supervisors who are sensitive to the problems of women and who can guide women students for the ministry in a sound and liberating approach to these problems. Finally and most importantly, she should arrange for the placement of women students in field education in those areas in which they experience the most acute forms of discrimination.

CONCLUSION

In order to carry out the important goals outlined in this proposal, it is evident that adequate funds will be needed. We have stressed the importance of the problem with which it deals. This will be the first program of major proportion in this country. Moreover, and significantly, it will be located in one of the great theological centers of the world. The program is extremely timely since it comes at the moment of the emergence of the women's liberation movement. For these reasons those who have drawn up the proposal stress the importance of the planned program and the necessity of adequate funding.

Unfortunately, as yet few persons have come to recognize the magnitude of the problem of women and the church. Funds are being made available for all sorts of causes . . . yet what cause could be more essential than the humanizing of the man-woman relationship in and through the agency of the church? Those who support this project will be in the forefront not only of the women's liberation movement, but also of the more universal movement toward human liberation.

SELECTED BIBLIOGRAPHY

BIBLIOGRAPHIES

Cisler, Lucinda. "Women: A Bibliography." A 14-category annotated reading list of 600 items, 16 pages long. Available by mail from Lucinda Cisler, 102 West 80th Street, New York, N. Y. 10024.

Jacquet, Constant H. "The Professional Woman in the United States: A Bibliographical Essay," Information Service, May 31, 1969. Published by the Department of Research, National Council of Churches, 475 Riverside Drive, New York, New York 10027.

WOMEN

Buytendijk, F. J. J. *Woman: A Contemporary View*. Translated by Denis J. Barrett. New York: Newman Press and Association Press, 1968.

de Beauvoir, Simone. *The Second Sex*. Translated by H. M. Parshley. New York: Alfred A. Knopf, 1953.

————. *The Woman Destroyed*. New York: G. P. Putnam's Sons, 1969.

Ellman, Mary. *Thinking About Women*. New York: Harcourt, Brace and World, 1968.

Flexner, Eleanor. *Century of Struggle*. Cambridge: Harvard University Press, 1959.

Hays, H. R. *The Dangerous Sex: The Myth of Feminine Evil*. New York: Putnam, 1964.

Kraditor, Aileen S. *The Ideas of the Woman Suffrage Movement*. New York: Columbia University Press, 1965.

————. *Up From the Pedestal*. Chicago: Quadrangle Books, 1968.

Lifton, Robert Jay, ed. *The Woman in America*. Boston: Houghton-Mifflin, The Daedalus Library, 1965. (Also *Daedalus* magazine, Spring, 1964.)

Mead, Margaret. *Male and Female*. New York: Apollo, 1968.

Mills, John Stuart. *The Subjection of Women*. New York: Stokes, 1911.

O'Neill, William L. *Everyone Was Brave: The Rise and Fall of Feminism in America*. Chicago: Quadrangle Press, 1969.

Parker, Elizabeth. *The Seven Ages of Woman*. Baltimore: Johns Hopkins Press, 1960.

Reik, Theodore. *Creation of Woman: A Psychological Inquiry into the Myth of Eve*. New York: Braziller, 1960.

Theobald, Robert, ed. *Dialogue on Women.* New York: Bobbs-Merrill Co., Inc., 1967.

WOMEN'S LIBERATION

It would be impossible to cite here all the material which has appeared in recent years in connection with the Women's Liberation Movement. Those listed here are a sample of the most recent books by the women of the movement. Periodical literature is extensive and should be available to almost any reader.

Bird, Caroline. *Born Female: The High Cost of Keeping Women Down.* New York: David McKay, 1968.

Epstein, Cynthia Fuchs. *Woman's Place.* Los Angeles: University of California Press, 1970.

Friedan, Betty. *The Feminine Mystique.* New York: Norton, 1963.

Kennedy, Florynce, and Diane Schulder. *Abortion Rap.* New York: McGraw-Hill, 1970.

Millet, Kate. *Sexual Politics.* New York: Doubleday and Co., 1970.

Morgan, Robin. *Sisterhood Is Powerful: An Anthology of Writings from Women's Liberation.* New York: Random House, 1970.

Thompson, Mary Lou. *Voices of New Feminism.* Boston: Beacon Press, 1970.

Additional resources may be secured from:

National Organization for Women, 250 West 57th Street, New York, N.Y. 10022.

Resource Center on Women's Liberation, YWCA, 650 Lexington Avenue, New York, N.Y. 10022. Helen Southard, Director.

The Women's Center, 36 West 22nd Street, New York, N.Y. 10011.

WOMEN IN THE CHURCH

A complete bibliography of women in the church is desperately needed. Sources are scattered and much of the valuable uncatalogued early material is lost or generally unknown. This list concentrates on recent works and attempts to present varied viewpoints on the issue. It is intended only to be representative and to assist those who may wish to pursue further the questions raised in this book. Omissions are not necessarily intentional; however, since a fair amount of what has been written in the past had the intention of praising and preserving the

*status quo with regard to the participation of women in the church,
some titles are notably absent.*

Achtemeier, Elizabeth. *Feminine Crisis in Christian Faith.* Nashville:
Abingdon Press, 1965.

Ashbrook, J. B. "The Church as a Matriarchy." *Pastoral Psychology,*
Vol. 14 (Spring 1963), pp. 38–49.

Bachofen, Johann J. *Myth, Religion and Mother Rights.* Translated by
R. Manheim. Princeton, N.J.: Princeton University Press, 1967.

Bacon, F. D. *Women in the Church.* London: Lutterworth, 1945.

Bailey, D. S. *The Man-Woman Relationship in Christian Thought.* London: Longmans, 1959.

Barot, Madelaine. *Cooperation of Men and Women in Church, Family
and Society.* Geneva: World Council of Churches, 1964.

Beaton, Catherine. "Does the Church Discriminate Against Women on
the Basis of Their Sex?" *Critic,* June-July, 1966, pp. 21–27.

Bliss, Kathleen. *The Service and Status of Women in the Churches.*
London: SCM Press, Ltd., 1952.

Calkins, Grace Gilkey. *Follow Those Women.* New York: United
Church Women, 1961.

Callahan, Sidney Cornelia. *Beyond Birth Control: Christian Experience
of Sex.* New York: Sheed and Ward, 1968.

———. *The Illusion of Eve.* New York: Sheed and Ward, 1965.

Cavert, Inez M. "Status of Women in the Local Church." *Pastoral Psychology,* Vol. 4, no. 34 (May 1953).

"Changing Roles of Men and Women in Contemporary Culture." In
Man in Community, Council for Lay Life and Work, United
Church of Christ, October 1965.

Church Woman, The, Church Women United, published monthly.

Concern, United Presbyterian Women, published monthly. See especially November 1964, *entire issue.*

Concerning the Ordination of Women. Geneva: World Council of
Churches, 1964.

Cooper, John. "St. Paul's Evaluation of Women and Marriage." *Lutheran Quarterly,* Vol. 16 (1964), pp. 291–302.

Cox, Harvey. "Sex and Secularization." In *The Secular City.* New York:
Macmillan, 1965.

Crook, Margaret. *Women and Religion.* Boston: Beacon Press, 1965.

Culver, Elsie Thomas. *Women in the World of Religion.* Garden City,
N.Y.: Doubleday and Co., 1967.

Cunneen, Sally. *Sex: Female; Religion: Catholic.* New York: Holt,
Rinehart and Winston, 1968.

Daly, Mary. *The Church and the Second Sex.* New York: Harper and
Row, 1968.

————. "The Forgotten Sex: A Built-in Bias." *Commonweal,* January 15, 1965, p. 41.

Danielou, Jean, S.J. *Ministry of Women in the Early Church.* London: The Faith Press, Ltd., 1961.

Douglas, William. *Ministers' Wives.* New York: Harper and Row, 1965.

————. "Women in the Church: Historical Perspectives and Contemporary Dilemmas." *Pastoral Psychology.* Vol. 12, no. 115 (June 1961), pp. 13–20.

Dumas, Francine. *Man and Woman: Similarity and Difference.* Translated by Margaret House. Geneva: World Council of Churches, 1966.

Ermarth, Margaret. *Adam's Fractured Rib.* Philadelphia: Fortress Press, 1970.

Faherty, William B. "God and the Single Girl." *Cross and Crown,* Vol. 17, June 15, 1966, pp. 134–142.

Farians, Elizabeth. "The Human Dignity of Women in the Church." Ecumenical Task Force on Women and Religion, National Organization for Women, 1424 16th Street, N.W., Washington, D.C. 20036.

————. "The Status of Women in the Church." Ecumenical Task Force on Women and Religion, National Organization for Women.

————. "Women in the Church Now." Ecumenical Task Force on Women and Religion, National Organization for Women.

Foster, Hazel. "The Ecclesiastical Status of Women," *The Woman's Pulpit,* Vol. 45, no. 4 (October-December, 1967), pp. 7–10.

Foye, Edward. "Androgynous Church." *Front Line,* September 1967, *entire issue.*

Gibson, Elsie. *When the Minister is a Woman.* New York: Holt, Rinehart and Winston, 1970.

Goldstein, Valerie S. "The Human Situation: A Feminine Viewpoint." *Journal of Religion,* Vol. 40 (April 1960), pp. 100–112.

Henrichsen, Margaret. *Seven Steeples.* Boston: Houghton-Mifflin Co., 1953.

Herschberger, Ruth. *Adam's Rib.* New York: Pellegrini and Cudahy, 1948. (Out of print.)

Hunter, Doris and Howard. "Neither Male nor Female." *Christian Century,* Vol. 82 (April 28, 1965), p. 527 ff.

Journal of Pastoral Psychology, December 1967, *entire issue.*

Kelly, Sister Suzanne. "Putting Sisters in Their Place." *America,* Vol. 114, January 1, 1966, pp. 10–11. (For letters in reply to this article, see March 5, 1966 issue, pp. 329–330.)

Krebs, A. V. "A Church of Silence." *Commonweal,* July 10, 1964, p. 472.

Lauer, Rosemary. "Women and the Church." *Commonweal,* December 20, 1963, pp. 365–68.

Lindbeck, Violette. "Ordination of Women." *Salt,* Philadelphia: Lutheran Press, Spring, 1967.

———. "Protestantism and Singleness." *The Church Woman,* February 1967, pp. 3–9.

McKenna, Sister Mary Lawrence. *Women of the Church: Role and Renewal.* New York: P.J. Kenedy and Sons, 1967.

McKinnon, Alastair T. "Women and the Church: The Real Issue." *Christian Outlook,* Vol. 16, no. 2, December 1960, Montreal.

Maertens, Thierry. *The Advancing Dignity of Woman in the Bible.* Translated by Sandra Dibbs. De Pere, Wisconsin: St. Norbert Abbey Press, 1969.

Moll, Will. *Christian Image of Women.* Chicago: Fides, 1967.

Murray, Pauli. "Women's Liberation—Pattern for the 70's?" *The Church Woman,* January 1970, pp. 11–14.

Nyberg, Kathleen Neill. *The New Eve.* Nashville: Abingdon Press, 1967.

"On the Liberation of Women." *Motive* magazine, March-April 1969, *entire issue.*

"Ordain Women?" *The Woman's Pulpit,* July-September, 1967, p. 4.

Prohl, Russell. *Women in the Church.* Grand Rapids, Michigan: Eerdmans, 1957.

Rankin, Robert Parks. "The Ministerial Calling and the Minister's Wife." *Pastoral Psychology,* September, 1960, pp. 16–22.

Ruether, Rosemary. "The Becoming of Women in Church and Society." *Crosscurrents,* Vol. 17 (Fall, 1967), pp. 418–426.

Ritchie, Jeanne. "Church, Caste and Women." *Christian Century,* Vol. 87, no. 3, January 21, 1970, pp. 73–77. (For letters in response to this article, see March 11, 1970 issue, pp. 295–298.)

Royden, Maude. *The Church and Woman.* London: James Clarke and Co., Ltd, n.d.

Ryrie, Charles Caldwell. *The Place of Women in the Church.* Chicago: Moody Press, 1968.

Sign magazine, October 1966, *entire issue.*

Sign magazine, August 1970, *entire issue.*

Sullivan, Dan. "Sex and the Person." *Commonweal,* July 22, 1966, p. 12.

Stendahl, Krister. *The Bible and the Role of Women.* Philadelphia: Fortress Press, 1966.

Suthers, Hanna B. "Religion and the Feminine Mystique." *Christian Century,* Vol. 82, June 30, 1965, pp. 911–914.

Tavard, George. "Women in the Church: A Theological Problem?" *The Ecumenist,* November-December, 1965, p. 51.

Way, Peggy. "The Church and [Ordained] Women." *The Christian Ministry,* January 1970, pp. 18–22.

Wedel, Cynthia. *Employed Women and the Church.* National Council of Churches, 1959.

"Woman." *The Chicago Theological Seminary Register,* Vol. 60, no. 3 (March 1970), *entire issue.*

"Woman Intellectual and the Church: A Symposium, The." *Commonweal,* January 27, 1967, pp. 446–459.

Woman's Pulpit, The. Des Moines: American Association of Women Ministers. Published quarterly.

"Women and the Church." *Renewal* magazine, October 1964, *entire issue.*

"Women's Place in the Church." *New World Outlook,* Vol. 30, no. 77 (July 1970), pp. 19–22.

"World Around Us: Liberation Struggle Generates Tension on Race, Sex Issues." *Christian Century,* Vol. 87, no. 23, June 10, 1970, pp. 736–742.

Wyker, Mossie. *Church Women in the Scheme of Things.* St. Louis: Bethany Press, 1953.

————. "The Role of Women in Religious Organizations." United Church of Christ.

Visser't Hooft, Henriette. "Cohumanity and the Covenant." *Theology Today,* Vol. 19, April 1962, pp. 71–74.

NOTES ON THE CONTRIBUTORS

SUSAN COPENHAVER BARRABEE completed her undergraduate education at Drake University in Des Moines, Iowa. She is currently enrolled in the Master of Divinity program at Drew Theological School, where her husband is on the faculty. In the fall, with the aid of a grant from Auburn Theological Seminary and the Women's Division of the Board of Missions of the United Methodist Church, she and Nelle Morton will begin research on the problems facing women in suburbia.

SIDNEY CORNELIA CALLAHAN combines the role of journalist and lecturer with that of wife and mother. She received her B.A. from Bryn Mawr College and is currently completing a master's degree in psychology from Sarah Lawrence College. She is the author of *The Illusion of Eve, Beyond Birth Control: Christian Experience of Sex,* and *How to Work and Be a Good Mother* (Macmillan, 1971). Active as a laywoman in church reform activities, she serves as a consultant to Family Life and Confraternity of the Christian Doctrine Office in the Archdiocese of New York.

DAVIDA FOY CRABTREE was graduated from Marietta College and is presently studying for the Bachelor of Divinity degree at Andover-Newton Theological Seminary. She was active in the United Church of Christ as a high school student and is now a member of the caucus of the Massachusetts Conference and a vice-president-at-large of the National Council of Churches. In addition she is active in the Women's Liberation Movement in the Boston area and participated in the planning of a proposed center for women at Boston Theological Institute. An article by her on Anne Hutchinson appeared in the September issue of the *Andover-Newton Quarterly.*

NORMA RAMSEY JONES was graduated from Centre College of Kentucky and holds a Bachelor of Divinity degree from Princeton University. She recently completed a master's degree in English literature at Bowling Green University and is working on a doctorate with a specialty in fiction by black American writers. As an ordained minister in the United Presbyterian Church of the USA she has served as pastor of a church in Amesville, Ohio and as an assistant pastor of the First Presbyterian Church of Bowling Green, Ohio.

ROSEMARY RADFORD RUETHER is Professor of Historical Theology in the School of Religion at Howard University. As an active and outspoken Roman Catholic lay theologian her writings have appeared in numerous religious periodicals. Her published works include: *The Church Against Itself; Communion is Life Together; Gregory of Nazianzus: Rhetor and Philosopher;* and most recently, *The Radical Kingdom.*

THE SISTERS OF THE IMMACULATE HEART OF MARY were established in 1924 as the California Institute of the Sisters of the Most Holy and Immaculate Heart of the Blessed Virgin Mary. In 1970, after three years of controversy with the Vatican Congregation for Religious, members of the order were granted dispensation from their canonical vows to form "a lay community of religious persons" in keeping with the principles of renewal which they had first outlined for themselves in 1967.

PEGGY ANN WAY holds a Bachelor of Divinity degree from Chicago Theological Seminary and is an ordained minister in the United Church of Christ. In past years she was co-pastor with her husband of a local church, taught at two seminaries and worked with the Chicago City Missionary Society. She is presently assistant Professor, Director of Metropolitan Ministries, at the University of Chicago Divinity School and is serving as national chairman of the Council for Church and Ministry of the United Church of Christ. She has published articles in *The Christian Ministry, Christian Century* and other religious periodicals.